JAMESTOWN ARCHAEOLOGY

This book showcases the latest information and newly discovered seventeenth-century artifacts from Jamestown, Virginia, the first permanent English settlement in America.

Jamestown Archaeology: Remains To Be Seen uses archaeological discoveries to greatly augment what we know about the settlement from written records. It discusses how the archaeological revelations recreate the backdrop where, amid Jamestown's growing fortifications, its houses, government buildings, churches, graves and village streets, the rule of law, representative democratic government, and venture capitalism took root in America. The volume examines the archaeological discoveries that date from the time of the first fortifications (James Fort 1607–1624) to the middle of the eighteenth century. It includes a chapter devoted specifically to how the fort was built, then redesigned and enlarged. It also addresses the archaeological examination of sites and artifacts relating to the Virginia Indians including a discussion of Pocahontas and the location of her lost grave in England. The 1676 "Bacon's" Rebellion is explored along with various episodes of destruction and the building of the first Virginia Capitol building, the Ludwell Statehouse Complex. The last chapter presents a comparative review of Jamestown Island maps drawn every century since the town was founded showing photographically and cartographically how much of the Island and its archaeological sites have been lost to erosion and rising water for 400 years, ending with thoughts about the need for rescuing sites today in the face of climate change, sea level rise, and more Island land erosion.

This book is for historical archaeologists and historians as well as readers with an interest in the beginnings of America.

Dr. William M. Kelso is the former Director of Archaeology for the Jamestown Rediscovery Foundation. He holds a Master's Degree in Early American History from the College of William and Mary, and a Ph.D. from Emory University. In 2012, Queen Elizabeth II named him (Hon.) Commander of the British Empire (CBE). He has authored books including *Archaeology at Monticello* (1994); *Jamestown, The Buried Truth* (2006); and *Jamestown, The Truth Revealed* (2017).

JAMESTOWN ARCHAEOLOGY

Remains To Be Seen

William M. Kelso

Routledge
Taylor & Francis Group

LONDON AND NEW YORK

Designed cover image: Ruins of Jamestown

First published 2024
by Routledge
4 Park Square, Milton Park, Abingdon, Oxon OX14 4RN

and by Routledge
605 Third Avenue, New York, NY 10158

Routledge is an imprint of the Taylor & Francis Group, an informa business

© 2024 William M. Kelso

The right of William M. Kelso to be identified as author of this work has been asserted in accordance with sections 77 and 78 of the Copyright, Designs and Patents Act 1988.

British Library Cataloguing-in-Publication Data
A catalogue record for this book is available from the British Library

ISBN: 978-1-032-57936-8 (hbk)
ISBN: 978-1-032-57934-4 (pbk)
ISBN: 978-1-003-44167-0 (ebk)

DOI: 10.4324/9781003441670

Typeset in Times New Roman
by KnowledgeWorks Global Ltd.

CONTENTS

FIGURES

ACKNOWLEDGMENTS

The achievements of the Jamestown Rediscovery® project at Historic James-towne®, Virginia, are due in large measure to the many individuals and organizations who have provided leadership, generous financial support, scholarly advice, and expertise.

Among the hundreds who could be acknowledged, I highlight a few here for special recognition: The Jamestown Rediscovery National Advisory Board, especially chairman Dr. Warren M. Billings, Dennis B. Blanton, DR. Carter Hudgins, Dr. Edward Bond, Frederick Faust, Dr. Jeffrey P. Brain, Dr. Cary Carson, Dr. Kathleen Deegan, Dr. Rex M. Ellis, Dr. Alaric Faulkner, Dr. William W. Fitzhugh, Ms. Camille Hedrick, Dr. James Horn, Dr. Jon Kukla, Dr. Douglas Owsley, Dr. David Orr, Mr. Oliver Perry, Dr. Carmel Schrire, Dr. George Stuart, Dr. Sandra Treadway, Dr. Edwin Randolph Turner, Mr. Robert Wharton, and Ms. Roxanne Gilmore; APVA Preservation Virginia's Trustees, Executive Director Elizabeth S. Kostelny, Jamestown Rediscovery President James Horn, and our special partner, the National Park Service. Generous benefactors to recognize include the U.S. Congress, the Commonwealth of Virginia, National Geographic Society, National Endowment for the Humanities, Virginia Foundation for the Humanities, James City County, City of Williamsburg, the Mellon Foundation, the Mary Morton Parsons Foundation, Jessie Ball DuPont Fund, 1772 Foundation, the Morgan Foundation, an anonymous Richmond foundation, the Garden Club of Virginia, the William Byrd and Colonial Capital Branches of the APVA, the Beirne Carter Foundation, Anheuser-Busch, Dominion Resources, Universal Leaf Corporation, Wachovia, Verizon, the William M. Grover Jr. family, Mr. Ivor Massey Jr., Mr. and Mrs. Peter I. C. Knowles II, Mr. and Mrs. John H. Guy IV, Mr. and Mrs. D. Anderson Williams, Mr. and Mrs. John A. Prince, the Alan M. Voorhees Family, Mrs. T. Eugene Worrell, the Edward Maria Wingfield Family Society, the Fontaine

C. Stanton Estate, William G. Beville, Mr. and Mrs. John H. Van Landingham III, Mr. and Mrs. Martin Kirwan King, and Mr. and Mrs. William Garber.

I am especially thankful to Patricia Cornwell's unflagging interest, generous funding, and unforgettable English research trips for the team through the years without which our archaeological James Fort search would have ended way too soon.

Also I am eternally grateful to Don and Elaine Bogus for their generous funding of archaeologists, for supporting the annual archaeological field school, for making the James Fort site come alive with on-site exhibits, for their major subvention for the publishing of this book, and for their steadfast encouragement of me personally over many years.

The project has been very much a staff team effort from the start and very much an experienced team effort. With an open mind to ways of improving the process, over the many years of the project the team has had an opportunity to fine-tune the way things have been done and I am especially grateful for their ability to decipher the ever-widening archaeological story at Historic Jamestowne. I am indebted to senior curators Bly Straube and Merry Outlaw for their unequaled and ever-expanding understanding of post-medieval material culture and for their disciplined and insightful reading of seventeenth-century Jamestown documents; former senior staff archaeologist Eric Deetz for his mastery of fieldwork, insight into post-medieval vernacular architecture, and education of students and visitors; senior staff archaeologist and graphic artist Jamie May for her skillful field work, her exceptional artistic eye for organizing and creating our interpretive illustrations, maps, site interpretation and images for this publication and for our many museum exhibits; and senior archaeologist Mary Anna Hartley for her exceptional skillful reading of archaeological signs in the soil; Danny Schmidt for his tenacious and ever enthusiastic fieldwork, his steadfast dedication to archiving field data, and for organizing and contributions to our technical reports; Carter Hudgins for his exceptional communication and field skills; Lee McBee for his remarkable ability to teach visitors; the late Dan Boyd Smith for his interpretive insight and commitment to the archives and historical research, information technologist Dave Givens for his insight into Virginia Indian archaeology and for creating our GIS archives; conservator/photographer Michael Lavin for his uniquely experienced conservation touches and photographic eye; Dan Gamble and Don Warmke for their ever-diligent and talented conservation work; and to the many, many skill archaeologists along the way for their diligent and talented fieldwork, especially Nick Luccketti, Luke Peccarero, Seth Mallios, Sarah Stroud, Heather Lapham, and original conservator and information technologist Elliott Jordan; and Dr. Douglas W. Owsley, Chief Anthropologist at the Smithsonian Institution, and Kari Bruwelheide for their exceptional scholarship and teaching me about careful forensic science. I am also grateful for the exceptional fund-raising efforts of Denise Kellogg. The efforts of the University of Virginia annual field school students are especially recognized. I am also especially grateful for the stalwart and always encouraging corps of Historic Jamestowne interpreters and the field and lab volunteers.

And I am forever indebted to Ivor Noël Hume for first revealing to me the rigorous process of historical archaeology, the thrill of archaeological discovery, and the archaeological possibilities at Jamestown. Without the original support of past APVA president Mary Douthat Higgins and Shirley Van Landingham, the rediscovery of Jamestown would never have happened.

PREFACE

This is the third book presenting my own interpretation of seventeenth-century archaeological remains found at Jamestown, Virginia, the first permanent English settlement in America (*Jamestown The Buried Truth 2006, Jamestown The Truth Revealed, 2017*)*. It is about the unearthing of things last touched by people four centuries ago, producing a sense of realism of who they were and what they did. I explain my view of how these discoveries add a powerful third dimension to the conventional interpretation of the story most people thought was already known about Jamestown from written records alone. Further, I discuss how archaeological revelations recreate the backdrop where, amid Jamestown's growing fortifications, its houses, government buildings, churches, graves and village streets, the rule of law, representative democratic government, and venture capitalism first took root in America. Further, I add to these revelations with an examination of the physical effects on the town of a violent but failed insurrection which tested the staying power of the fledgling democracy. At the same time, I recognize that the discovery of artifacts and building remains recreate the place from which the English first launched a militant policy of conquering traditional Indian lands. And I present my vision of the town where the English practice of enslaving for life forcefully imported Africans began and flourished. In other words, this volume is my look at the once-buried evidence of the place where America first struggled to invent itself.

More specifically, this volume examines my own conclusions about some of the archaeological discoveries that date from the time of the first fortifications (James Fort 1607–1624) to the middle of the eighteenth century. It includes my interpretation of evidence about how James Fort was built, then redesigned and enlarged. I also briefly address the archaeological of evidence of Virginia Indian women that suggests they were surprisingly living in the fort and discuss one of them, the "Indian Princess" Pocahontas, and her much-fabled burial location. My reading of finds postdating the early fort such as archaeological evidence of the fiery impact of the 1676 "Bacon's" Rebellion and the burning of two private buildings: the John White Warehouse and the William Drummond House and two public structures: the Brick Church and the Virginia Statehouse. This includes my reading of the identity of some burials found in the reconstructed church and the surprising find in the churchyard of a government official's burial, a man who owned part of Statehouse buildings and redesigned his residence there. Finally, I offer my comparative review of Jamestown Island maps drawn every century since the town was founded showing photographically and cartographically how much of the Island and its archaeological sites have been lost to 400 years of rising water. I end the book with my plea for rescuing sites today in the face of climate change, sea level rise, and the consequential erosion of more Island land.

*Dr. William M. Kelso, (Hon.) CBE, FSA, former Director of Archaeology, Jamestown Rediscovery Foundation, 1993–2021. 6/2/2023.

1

A JAMESTOWN DOCUMENTARY

> The soil was good and fruitful, with excellent good timber. There are also great store of vines in bigness of a man's thigh, running up to the tops of the trees, in great abundance ... many squirrels, conies, blackbirds with crimson wings and divers other fowls and birds of divers and sundry colors of crimson, watchet, yellow, green, murrey and of divers other hues naturally without any art using.[1]

The description given above of the Virginia wonderland came from the pen of George Percy, one of the first Jamestown settlers, who was to become governor of the colony almost by default when the dreamland turned into a nightmare two and one-half years later. Percy's account of the voyage to the New World is the most complete of the firsthand descriptions of the founding of Jamestown and the fate of the colonists during the first spring and summer in Virginia.

Eyewitness testimonies carry great weight in any search for the truth. A reading of the documents pertaining to early Jamestown is essential if we are to discover its buried secrets. But documents must be read carefully: the testimony even of eyewitnesses must be scrutinized, keeping in mind that the authors were not immune to dreams of gold and glory that might distort their accounts. It is important to ask, for instance, how much of the fruitful abundance Percy describes in his first sighting might have been merely an expression of the hopes of a new settler rather than reality.

An examination of the documents contemporary with Jamestown's founding offers hints of the precise location, configuration, and artifacts of James Fort. In all, only a half dozen firsthand descriptions and two maps survive from the earliest

DOI: 10.4324/9781003441670-1

FIGURE 1.1   George Percy, highest ranking original settler and lieutenant governor 1609–1610.

Source: By Herbert Luther Smith (Virginia Historical Society, Richmond).

years of the colony to guide an archaeologist's shovels and trowels. Here are the salient facts about the writers of these documents:

John Smith:	Arrived in Jamestown 1607. Yeo-man farmer's son, mariner, and soldier, often at odds with his less-experienced and higher-born colleagues. From 1608 to 1631, he published varying accounts of his 29 months in Virginia, as well as heavily edited reports written by other settlers who stayed on. His sometimes-inconsistent accounts sought to justify his actions at Jamestown as well as promote colonization.
Gabriel Archer:	Arrived in Jamestown 1607. Mariner and explorer, trained in the law. As recording secretary for the Virginia governing council, he described the earliest days of

FIGURE 1.2   Captain John Smith.

Source: By Simon de Passe (Library of Virginia).

	Jamestown in what appear to be official reports sent back to the Company in England. A devoted enemy of John Smith, he died during the "starving time" of 1609–1610.
George Percy:	Arrived in Jamestown 1607. Son of the earl of Northumberland, Percy was one of the highest-ranked of the colonists on the social scale. He served as stand-in governor during the "starving time" and was reappointed in 1611. Percy wrote an account of the 1606–1607 voyage from England and a refutation of Smith's 1624 *Generall Historie*, which had put much of the blame for the "starving time" on Percy's shoulders.
Ralph Hamor:	Arrived in Jamestown 1609. A stockholder in the Virginia Company, later a member of the governor's council in the

	1620s, he published an apparent promotional report in 1615, describing a flourishing Jamestown in 1611–1614, urging further investment and emigration.
William Strachey:	Arrived in Jamestown 1609. Secretary of the colony. His letter of 1610 includes an account of the colony as he saw it in May–July 1610 and a summary of earlier events, which Percy apparently dictated to him. The most polished of the early reporters, he wrote the most exact description of James Fort, but his reliance on Percy casts some doubt on the accuracy of his account of Jamestown's first three years.
"The Ancient Planters of Virginia":	Writing in the spring of 1623, these surviving original settlers thought the Crown should know about the mishandling of the colony under the leadership of the Virginia Company treasurer, Sir Thomas Smythe. Although cast to shed ill light on Smythe, the account includes details about Jamestown houses and hardships during the early years.
Don Pedro de Zúñiga:	The Zúñiga map of Virginia was delivered to King Philip III of Spain in 1608 by his ambassador to England, Don Pedro de Zúñiga. This is believed by some to be a tracing of an early map by John Smith. The map includes a minuscule sketch of James Fort. Zúñiga repeatedly urged King Philip to wipe out the colony.
Johannes Vingboons:	The Vingboons chart is a Dutch navigational chart showing structures on Jamestown Island as well as downriver forts, all in an area labeled "New Nederland."

The Fort

In May of 1607, Virginia looked like the Garden of Eden to Percy and probably to the 105 English "gentlemen, artisans, laborers and servant boys" seeking a place to settle in the name of King James I, and, more important, a place to reap profit for their investors, the Virginia Company of London. At this point, Virginia appeared to be what they expected: the ideal place to plant a permanent colony of English people, to find gold and a route to the rich Orient, and to convert the natives to Christianity. The Virginia Company officials had instructed the adventurers to settle at least 100 miles from the ocean, in a place where a major river narrowed, offering defensive positions on either side of any attacking ship—which would surely be Spanish, avenging past English privateering raids. As an alternative, the colonists were advised to settle "some Island that is strong by nature." Led by Newport and Wingfield, and following their instructions, the three ships entered the

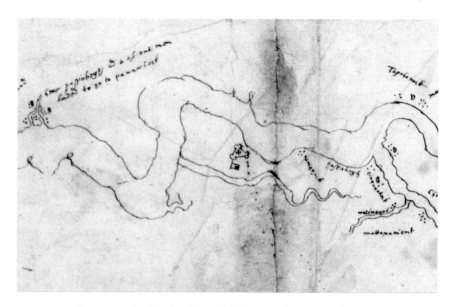

FIGURE 1.3   Known as the Zuniga Map (1608), one of the three known seventeenth-century renderings of James Fort.

Source: Monisterio de Educacion y Cultura de Espana, Achivo General de Simancas, MPD.19.163.

largest river of the Chesapeake, which they named after their king. The party then sailed as far as 65 miles northwest looking for that defendable narrow stretch of river. Reaching the Appomattox River without having found an uninhabited place with the right requirements, the colonists turned back toward the bay. On May 13, the group decided to settle on a point of land that was actually an island at very high tide (Figures 1.3 and 1.4). Why there? Percy explained that here the channel was so close to the shore that ships could be tied to the trees.[3] Other considerations made Jamestown Island the settlement site of choice. Again, the Virginia Company's instructions came into play: the colonists were not to upset the Virginia Indians, especially by settling on land they already occupied. Jamestown Island was vacant. Although the island was a mere 35 miles from the open ocean, from which the Spanish could launch an attack, it still qualified as a naturally defensible place, with its narrow neck of land to guard against assault from the mainland Indians and its naturally hidden location in a sharp bend in the river.

The several ridges at Jamestown Island provided ideal sites for a fort, particularly the third ridge from the west, the highest point of land on the north shore of the river bend. It is also possible that, although the Indians did not then occupy the land, they had been there in the not-too-distant past. By 1607, their cleared land might have evolved into a fair-sized grove of straight, tall, second-growth hardwood trees, ideal for building timber palisades and blockhouses. Captain John Smith deemed Jamestown Island a very fit place for the erecting of a great city.

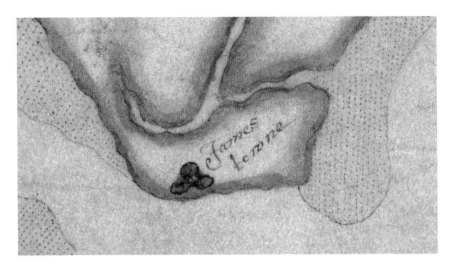

FIGURE 1.4   Tindall Map of Virginia, 1608, the earliest map of James Fort.

Source: The British Library.

FIGURE 1.5   Jamestown Island from the west.

Source: Jamestown Rediscovery Foundation, JRF.

The next day, the colonists—all men—filed ashore, on to what the English adventurers decided to call Jamestown Island on the north shore of the James River. That first landing day, Smith reports that the island was a busy place, with the men doing what they needed to do for survival: clearing the land, establishing shelter, preparing to live off their own gardens and the native fish, and fortifying themselves despite Company instructions not to upset the Indians by doing so. Like Smith, chronicler George Percy tells of throwing up a brush fort. Percy also writes of establishing a military guard. This exercise was wisely done. The settlers soon were challenged by the Paspahegh Indians from the nearest village.

Arriving with a hundred men in arms—a message that the English soldiers were essentially outnumbered and surrounded—the Indian leader "made signs that he would give us as much land as we would desire." Of course, the settlers already believed they had ownership by the English king's patent of the whole of continental North America. In any case, they must have rapidly accepted the offer, surely one that meant no more than the 1,600-acre Jamestown Island. But the deal seemed to go sour when one of the Indians grabbed a soldier's hatchet, prompting a scuffle in which a native was struck on the arm. The chief and his warriors left in anger.

The Indians seemed to be a forgiving lot, for 2 days later 40 appeared at the Jamestown "quarter" with a deer. In addition, they offered to stay in the "fort" all night. Sensing ambush, the English denied the overnight and proceeded to flaunt their own military prowess. They put on a demonstration to prove English weapons superior to the Indian arrows. They first set up a leather "target" (hand shield) for Indian target practice. An arrow penetrated a foot into the leather. Next, steel target went up which shattered. This set the stage for open warfare one week later.

On May 27, Captain Gabriel Archer described the first battle as a very furious assault on the fort by some 200 warriors. Wingfield, who presumably now knew the men would need more than brush and canvas to stay alive, ordered that the settlement be immediately and this time seriously fortified. According to Percy, on June 15 they had built and finished the fort, which was in the form of a triangle having three bulwarks at every corner and four or five pieces of artillery mounted in them. Building the fort was no easy task for such small numbers in so short a time. If cutting and hauling logs, probably weighing 800 pounds apiece, and digging at least 900 feet of trenches to seat them was not enough of a challenge, almost daily the workmen had to dodge Indian arrows shot from the surrounding woods and marsh grasses. The constant threat of incoming arrows, the heat of a developing Tidewater Virginia summer, and the stress of the fear-driven building schedule would eventually take its toll on the men.

In the days that followed, Percy chronicled the deaths of 25 colonists, including the councilor Bartholomew Gosnold. Later, Smith claims 67 were dead by September, but finally most of the soldiers recovered with the aid of master general surgeon, Thomas Wotton. The popular Captain John Smith took over as the colony's manager in September—President Wingfield having been impeached for allegedly hoarding food—Smith oversaw the building of some thatched houses. In the fall of 1607, a number of emissaries from James River Indian tribes expressed intentions of peace, and every four or five days Pocahontas (the great chief Powhatan's daughter, who had befriended Smith) and her attendants brought the men provisions. Despite these friendly actions, concern for security probably caused the new houses to be built inside the fort.

The exact form, size, and degree of sophistication of the council's fort cannot be determined from these early records, but it seems that much of the fort in its original configuration did not last long. In January 1608, after a supply ship and a hundred fresh men arrived from England, fire either seriously damaged or completely destroyed the fort. On top of that disaster, the winter of 1608 was one of extreme cold. That winter saw a rash of deaths, in which Smith reports that more than half of the men died. Despite these hardships, Smith reports a "rebuilding [of] James Towne," which included repairing the partially burned palisades, building the first substantial church, building a "Stove" (kitchen), and reroofing the storehouse—a first reference to the existence of the latter.

Whenever Smith returned to Jamestown from his explorations, once in July and again in September 1608, he wrote that he found the town in great decay and the men suffering and many dead, and the harvest rotting. In September, the council and company elected Smith president. Under his new leadership, further construction and an apparent redesign of the fort were carried out. Smith also restored discipline in the disorganized and disheartened militia. And when Captain Newport sailed back to England in late 1608, he carried among a cargo of clapboard and wainscot, Jamestown-made pitch, tar, glass, and soap-ashes.

In 1608–1609, Jamestown seemed to prosper under Captain John Smith's strict leadership. That spring, although Smith apparently found enough unspoiled food in the store to make it to the fall harvest, he wrote that he instituted a "must work or no food" policy to make sure, among other things, that there would be a harvest. But again, by the summer of 1609, the corn in the store rotted while the men planted 30 or 40 acres under the direction of the fettered Paspahegh prisoners Kemps and Tassore, who actually wanted to stay in the fort. And the settlers caught more of the giant and nutritious sturgeon which they transformed into bread. With that staple as well as various wild roots and fruits, according to Smith, all lived very well. But not for long. The same summer seven of a nine-ship supply flotilla made it in from England intending to revitalize the colony. Those ships also brought certain gentlemen who set out to murder Smith. Over 200 men took the new supplies away from Jamestown, going to live at the Falls of the James or downstream at the Nansemond River. When Smith sailed to the Falls in search of supplies in the late autumn, he returned with a life-threatening wound to his thigh caused by, as he put it, someone "accidentally" firing his powder bag. He soon decided to return to England and George Percy was named president.

In reporting the condition of the colony at the time of his departure, Smith's *Generall Historie* offers one of the most complete state-of-the-fort descriptions— one that of course made his tenure as president look positive:

> Leaving us with ... ten weeks' provision in the store, ... twenty-four pieces of ordinance, three hundred muskets, snaphaunces and firelocks, shot, powder, and match sufficient, curats [cuirasses], pikes, swords, and morio[n]s [helmets] more than men, an hundred well-trained and expert soldiers, nets for fishing, tools of all sorts to work, apparel to supply our wants, six mares and a horse, five or six hundred swine, some goats, some sheep ... . Jamestown was strongly palisadoed, containing more than fifty or sixty houses.[2]

But Smith also made clear his opinion that he was forced to leave behind the seeds of destruction, namely, poor gentlemen, tradesmen, serving men, and libertines (who Smith thought) were ten times more fit to spoil a commonwealth than either to begin one or help to maintain one. The 1609–1610 winter that followed became known as the "starving time." A flotilla of supply ships under the newly appointed lieutenant governor Sir Thomas Gates was shipwrecked in Bermuda. Indians besieged the fort. The colonists' livestock was quickly eaten, including the horses, and some of their weapons were traded away for Indian corn. Some of the "poorer sorte" even resorted to survival cannibalism. Only 60 of the 215 left at Jamestown survived.

By spring, the *Deliverance* and the *Patience,* replacements for the governor's wrecked flagship, the *Sea Venture,* arrived from Bermuda to find the palisades torn down, the ports open, the gates off their hinges, and empty houses. Lieutenant Governor Gates was accompanied by William Strachey, who began his relatively precise record of Jamestown's events and appearance in 1610. The supplies brought in from Bermuda soon disappeared, and the expectation of resupply from the Indians proved to be wishful thinking. The situation declined so badly that Gates ordered an evacuation of the town. With 30 days' supply, the survivors sailed downriver. Soon the evacuees met an advance party from the incoming supply fleet of the new governor, Thomas West, Lord De La Warre. After only 30 hours' respite from Jamestown, the demoralized group had to backtrack and prepare for the new governor's arrival. Thereafter, the new leadership and especially the new supplies quickly seemed to rejuvenate the town.

Secretary of the colony, William Strachey, described the condition of the fort as considerably more positive. Strachey observed,

> the fort growing since to more perfection, is now at this present in this manner: ... about half an acre ... is cast almost into the form of a triangle and so palisaded. The south side next the river (howbeit extended in a line or curtain sixscore foot more in length than the other two, by reason the advantage of the ground doth require) contains 140 yards, the west and east sides a hundred

FIGURE 1.6   Thomas West, Third Lord De La Warre, first resident governor of Virginia
1610–1611.

Source: Jamestown Settlement Foundation.

only. At every angle or corner, where the lines meet, a bulwark or watchtower
is raised and in each bulwark a piece or two well mounted... . And thus enclosed, as I said, round with a palisade of planks and strong posts, four feet
deep in the ground, of young oaks, walnuts, etc... . the fort is called, in honor
of His Majesty's name, Jamestown.[3]

Percy's and Strachey's descriptions agree that James Fort was triangular
with watchtowers and/or bulwarks at each of the three angles, where ordnance
was mounted. That design seems to be consistent with the two early maps, the
Tyndall Map and the Zuniga Map. The former shows the lower Chesapeake
Bay, the James and York Rivers, and the land between them from the Bay to
70 miles inland. The caption reads: "Draught of Virginia by Robarte Tindal

FIGURE 1.7   Sir Thomas Gates, lieutenant governor of Virginia 1610, 1611–1614.

Source: National Archives, Bermuda.

Anno 1608." Jamestown Island is drawn and labeled "Jamestown" and near the western end of the Island there are three circles attached by straight lines forming a triangle. This appears to be the James Fort plan described by Percy and Strachey. The Zuniga map shows a larger area including part of the eastern coast of modern North Carolina and much of Tidewater Virginia. It depicts "Jamestown" also basically in the form of a triangle, but the bulwarks at the angles are more complicated: two partial circles and an attached square form on the two river sides and only a relatively large circle to the north. The scale of both maps seems to defy any attempt at learning how far the fort was from the western end of the Island.

In 1611, after De La Warre's illness forced him to leave Jamestown, there arrived yet another Company-appointed governor, Sir Thomas Dale. That year, the optimistic settler Ralph Hamor described what seems to be a rather different Jamestown. His glowing account of a handsome town and rows of houses paints a picture of a renovated and expanded fortified area. Hamor never really says the town plan expanded outside the limits of the original fort in any particular direction, but he does mention houses scattered beyond the town. This handsome town, whatever its form, did apparently include a governor's residence, built by and for Lieutenant Governor Gates presumably when he took office in the summer of 1611. This building was expanded by other governors as they saw fit. The establishment of an official residence was a reflection of the 1609 Company charter, which vested both the commercial and the governmental affairs of the colony in the hands of the Company. Before then, the governing council, directed ultimately by the king himself, carried on the affairs of the colony.

There are no more detailed descriptions of James Fort/town, but there are hints that its development was an on-again, off-again process through the decade. Governors Gates and Dale, even though they kept their main residence at Jamestown (1611–1616), apparently let the fort slowly decay. Dale neglected Jamestown in favor of another fortified town he was building upriver at a place he called Henricus. Even before Dale's neglect, another document, if it states the truth, paints a Jamestown again in shambles by 1613. A Spanish prisoner held at Jamestown, Don Diego de Molina, smuggled a letter to the Spanish ambassador in London, urging a Spanish invasion of Virginia and a quick surrender of the disgruntled "slaves" at Jamestown, who were protected only by "fortifications … so fragile that a kick would destroy them … a fortification without skill and made by people who do not understand them."[4]

Things were no better in 1617 when yet another new lieutenant governor arrived at Jamestown, Captain Samuel Argall. Planter John Rolfe's disparaging description of the town is almost an echo of Gates's discovery of Jamestown just after the "starving time." Rolfe failed to mention that his own actions might have been in part responsible for Jamestown's decay. His development of a profitable tobacco strain that would thrive in Virginia soil had begun to drain the Jamestown population to hinterland tobacco plantations and diminished the settlers' interest in keeping up the fort—that is, except as they could grow tobacco in any vacant space there. Nevertheless, Argall set out to make things right by repairing the defective town. During his administration (1617–1619), a 20′ × 50′ church was built.

Also during Argall's tenure as governor, the Dutch were busy mapping Virginia, claiming it lay in "New Nederland"[5] (Figure 1.8). The area was so labeled on a circa-1617 detailed chart of the James River from its confluence with the Appomattox to the Chesapeake Bay. The map shows Jamestown Island, individual houses around modern Hopewell, and two other early Virginia forts: Fort Algernon at Point Comfort and Charles Fort at nearby Strawberry Bank. The downriver forts appear as attached gable-end buildings, three at Algernon and two at Charles Fort. Jamestown is depicted in an identical way—attached buildings—and located about one-third of the way from the western end of the island. The Dutch charts, intended

FIGURE 1.8   Detail of ca.1617 Dutch (Vingboons) chart of the James River showing Jamestown Island and vicinity.

Source: National Archives, The Hague, The Netherlands.

as navigational guides, usually show buildings as they would appear from a distant ship, not as mere symbolic structures. So either each of these forts had prominent multi-section storehouses or the chart symbols depict blockhouses or watchtowers, the most visible features of forts from a distance. In fact, the Jamestown Island buildings are labeled "Blockhouse Jamestown." If the triple houses mark the exact location of the town, as they almost certainly do, then the map locates the fort some distance from the now-eroded western end of the island.

Other documentary descriptions of James Fort's private and public buildings are vague but suggest that for months the town looked like a temporary army camp. As late as September 10, 1607, there were no houses, rotten tents, and shabby cabins. Three years later, however, things seemed to have improved some. Strachey described the houses in the fortified town:

> to every side, a proportioned distance from the palisade, is a settled street of houses that runs along so as each line of the angle hath his street … . builded though as yet no great uniformity, either for fashion or beauty … . The houses have wide and large country chimneys.[6]

There was a constant repair and replacement program: These so-called "cottages" may have been prone to decay but they were not scarce. By summer 1608, "we had about fortie or fiftie severall houses warm and dry." The town houses increased to 50 or 60 a year later. If the figure is not exaggerated, some of these houses had to stand outside the rather constrained space in the fort Strachey described.

There is very little record of James Fort after the Dutch navigators produced the 1617 chart. A last-minute warning saved the fort from damage during the disastrous Indian uprising of 1622. A year and a half later, James Fort, other forts, and a number of the houses in Virginia were all very much at risk.

This documentary evidence of the nature and extent of James Fort and the early town is often ambiguous. We know that much of this evidence could have been distorted for self-serving reasons. A 1623 document written by the "ancient planters" is significantly at odds with the earlier accounts. According to these surviving original settlers, in January 1608 the town only had 40 occupants, most dying, no houses, and lived in holes in the ground at the point of death—all utterly destitute of houses, not one as yet built, so that they lodged in cabins and holes in the ground. They do, however, mention the houses Gates constructed, presumably in 1611, that constant repair left still standing when the ancient planters wrote 12 years later.

Overall, a fairly consistent image emerges from these written accounts alone. James Fort was some sort of triangular enclosure, between one and two acres in size, built on ground located on the James River shore near the southwestern end of Jamestown Island. James Fort became Jamestown or James City soon in the literature; it included houses of varied quality, a church, a storehouse, and other buildings, and it grew in size. Many people died there from a number of causes, primarily disease, starvation, and battle with the Virginia Indians. The town had a number of episodes of neglect and decline, but each new governor's term brought the town back to serviceable condition or renovated and expanded it. The early fort fell into final decay and disappeared by 1624, when James I dissolved the Virginia Company and took over the colony for the crown.

The People

The eyewitness accounts of Jamestown's first 17 struggling years paint a picture not only of James Fort but also of the people involved in its founding—including the eyewitnesses themselves. Other available documentary evidence can tell us more of the events and people that affected the fabric of the developing Jamestown Island settlement. Demographic and biographical information can be gleaned from records of individual Englishmen who first landed there as well as of the people who came soon thereafter: the "diverse other" men and women. Their age, social standing, colonial and military experience, and place of origin in England all influenced how they reacted to the alien Virginia environment. Documents also tell of another people whose presence had a tremendous impact, both positively and negatively, on the siting and survival of Jamestown: the Virginia Indians who after all inhabited the land the English were invading. To a certain extent, they can be known individually, too.

Certain biographical facts are commonly known about some of the Jamestown leaders. We know, for example, something of the members of the first council selected by the Virginia Company before the voyage, their identities revealed at the opening of a sealed box containing a list of people preselected by the Company to rule the colony at the voyage's end: Edward Maria Wingfield, John Martin, Captain George Kendall, John Ratcliffe, Bartholomew Gosnold, and Captain John Smith. They all had military/combat experience acquired either in fighting the 80-year wars in the Netherlands, in privateering, or in establishing the English plantations in Ireland. Captain John Smith had fought not only in the Netherlands but also in France and Transylvania. Gosnold led the capture of a Spanish galleon and took a colonizing party to settle briefly off Cape Cod in 1602. Except for Smith, they all were gentry, some urban and some rural.

What is not so well known are their ages, which ranged from 27 (Smith) to 57 (Wingfield). The rest of the council were in their forties, except Gosnold, who was 36, and Kendall, 37. At a time when 56 was the average life expectancy, these men were primarily "seniors." (Thus, in his youth as well as in his lower social status, Smith did not fit the norm of the leaders.) The rest of the party for whom biographical data has been determined so far ranged in age from the 46-year-old Christopher Newport of Harwich to 9-year-old James Brumfield of Lincolnshire. The average age of the non-council men was about 25.[7]

The settlers' home parishes and probably their family seats were either the greater London area (including the Kent/Sussex counties to the southeast and Essex), Suffolk, the greater Peterborough area, or John Smith's Lincolnshire (Figure 1.9).

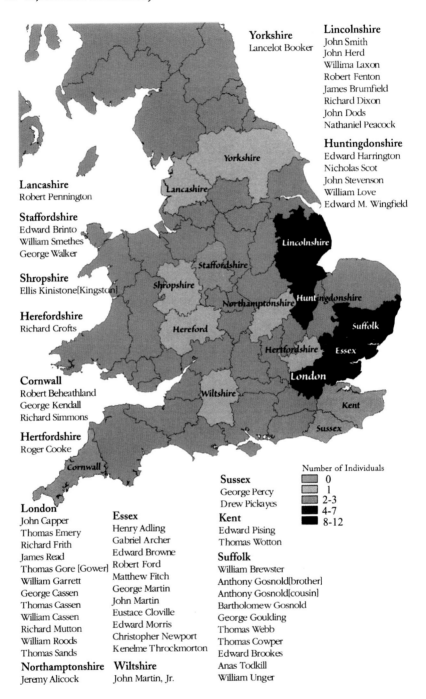

Yorkshire
Lancelot Booker

Lincolnshire
John Smith
John Herd
Willima Laxon
Robert Fenton
James Brumfield
Richard Dixon
John Dods
Nathaniel Peacock

Huntingdonshire
Edward Harrington
Nicholas Scot
John Stevenson
William Love
Edward M. Wingfield

Lancashire
Robert Pennington

Staffordshire
Edward Brinto
William Smethes
George Walker

Shropshire
Ellis Kinistone[Kingston]

Herefordshire
Richard Crofts

Cornwall
Robert Beheathland
George Kendall
Richard Simmons

Hertfordshire
Roger Cooke

Sussex
George Percy
Drew Pickayes

Number of Individuals
0
1
2-3
4-7
8-12

London
John Capper
Thomas Emery
Richard Frith
James Read
Thomas Gore [Gower]
William Garrett
George Cassen
Thomas Cassen
William Cassen
Richard Mutton
William Roods
Thomas Sands

Northamptonshire
Jeremy Alicock

Essex
Henry Adling
Gabriel Archer
Edward Browne
Robert Ford
Matthew Fitch
George Martin
John Martin
Eustace Cloville
Edward Morris
Christopher Newport
Kenelme Throckmorton

Wiltshire
John Martin, Jr.

Kent
Edward Pising
Thomas Wotton

Suffolk
William Brewster
Anthony Gosnold[brother]
Anthony Gosnold[cousin]
Bartholomew Gosnold
George Goulding
Thomas Webb
Thomas Cowper
Edward Brookes
Anas Todkill
William Unger

FIGURE 1.9 Map of southern England showing places of origin of a number of the first Jamestown colonists.

Source: Catherine Correll-Walls (Jamie May, JRF).

Of the original colonists whose place of origin can be determined, 12 came from the city of London, and an equal number came from the greater London area and East Anglia. Those from East Anglia—the river port town areas of Suffolk, Norfolk, Lincolnshire, and Cambridgeshire—were younger than those from the greater London area. A small percentage came from other towns or counties but not from any other single region in England. Fourteen came with relatives: cousins, fathers, sons, and brothers. Six had some kinship with Gosnold.

From these statistics, drawn from research still in progress, one might begin to speculate how and why these men and boys joined in the Virginia adventure. Finding gold was considered to be a realistic expectation, as was the assignment of land in Virginia to planters or the adventurers. It is logical to assume that many of the immigrants were the younger sons of gentry, with little prospect of inheriting the family lands in England. Insofar as we can now determine, at least six of the gentlemen were younger sons; the gentleman Bartholomew Gosnold, for example, had an older brother. Prospects for acquiring land in Virginia must have been appealing to these younger gentlemen, as to other immigrants well into the seventeenth century. But land could not have been the primary consideration for many others. At least three other gentlemen, including Wingfield and Martin, were the eldest sons in their families. Clearly, they were gentlemen with other motives, perhaps just the adventure of it all.

How did word of the voyage get out in an age when only one in ten could read and where the roads were hardly passable? The distribution patterns of geographic origins suggest that the principal leaders may have been the principal sources of information as well. It is logical to assume that the settlers from London learned of the venture through the promotional program of the Virginia Company based there. Thomas Smythe, the London merchant, whose wealth and influence played so large a part in the formation of the first Virginia Company and who may have had a personal hand in collecting the London recruits himself, was Bartholomew Gosnold's cousin-in-law.

Gosnold gathered the leaders and many of the other first settlers from among his East Anglian friends, neighbors, and relatives. He must have been a particularly effective promoter, since, like few others, he could describe firsthand the Atlantic voyage and at least part of the area then known as "Virginia." Gosnold would have been able to assure his listeners that the new Virginia adventure would be different. He had learned from the Norumbrian (New England) shortcomings and successes. He could well have said with conviction that the south of Virginia was a paradise in comparison to the northern latitudes. John Smith credited Gosnold with being the principal promoter of the Virginia venture.

By 1605, the plans for a southern colony led by Gosnold were much advanced, and by then included Wingfield, Gosnold's cousin Thomas Smythe, and Gosnold's friend, the soldier and traveler John Smith. In on the planning as well was Richard Hakluyt, the vicar of nearby All Saints Church, Weatheringsett, and the king's official geographer. It was Hakluyt who put into print the most vivid accounts of the English explorations in the New World and the most forceful and convincing arguments for founding English colonies. Judging from the way the East Anglian hometowns cluster on the map of southeastern England, it is logical to assume that Gosnold was an accomplished recruiter for the Virginia venture from the environs of Otley.

When the fleet sailed, however, Christopher Newport became the commanding admiral, and Wingfield, a chief stockholder in the Virginia Company, an aspiring president. As second-in-command despite his experience as a mariner, Gosnold must have watched helplessly as the fleet floundered in the mouth of the Thames for almost the entire first month of the voyage. Gosnold must also have been frustrated enduring Newport's long southern route to Virginia via the Canary and West Indian Islands when he already knew the benefit of the faster northern route.

We pick up the Jamestown story again in Virginia. After an unspecified illness of three weeks, the talented Gosnold died on August 22, 1607, and was buried in or near James Fort with full military honors. By the fall of 1607, according to Smith, 67 of the original 104 settlers had died, and George Percy recorded the deaths of 24 gentlemen, 1 laborer, and 2 others during the months of August and September 1607. The greatest number of the gentlemen, 11 of the 16 who were reported by Percy as having died, came from London. Others who died during the rest of the summer came from just about every other region in England. It is perhaps significant, however, that the men Captain John Smith took with him during his two voyages of "discovery" that summer, one to the Falls of the James and the other into the Chesapeake, included the men and boys from his home area of Lincolnshire and Norfolk. They were among those who apparently survived the summer death toll (or at least were not included in George Percy's list of the dead). Of course, they were away from Jamestown Island during the real heat of the summer, sailing on the open water, which gives more credence to the assumption that Jamestown Island with its marshes and lack of fresh spring water may have been responsible for the quick demise of so many. On the other hand, perhaps Smith chose the strongest and healthiest of the group to go with him, thus culling out the people who might have survived had they stayed at the fort.

The story of Jamestown traditionally focuses on Smith and other leaders, so much so that a number of people whose actions immeasurably affected the settlement become invisible. John Smith listed 213 settlers' names among those who made the first few Jamestown voyages, dismissing the rest as mere diverse others. These anonymous others should not be so quickly dismissed. Contributing just as significantly to the Jamestown story were hundreds of other unnamed colonists, both men and women.

The Virginia Indians' first significant impact was on the siting of Jamestown itself. Historians have long maligned the choice of the Jamestown site, owing to the unhealthy nature of the low-lying marshy island and the danger posed by the island's location deep within Powhatan's territory. The island is so low-lying today that 80 percent is below the water level of storm flooding. The lack of springs meant that only brackish river water or shallow wells could serve the colony, a fact often listed as contributing to Jamestown's high death rates. So why choose this place? Percy explained the choice by the proximity of the channel, but it is clear that the experienced military leaders saw the highest ground and the surrounding water as a natural defense against the expected enemies: the Virginia Indians and the Spanish.

To the natives themselves, "Virginia Indians" were neither "Virginian" nor "Indians." Those were their English names. In 1612, William Strachey, author of that precise James Fort description, wrote, "The severall territoryes and provinces which are in chief commaunded by their great king Powhatan, are comprehended under the denomynation of Tsenacommacoh, of which we may the more by experyence speak being the place wherein our abode and habitation hath now well neere six years consisted."[8] Tsenacomacah was the native name of the territory under the control of their leader, Powhatan, or at least that part of the territory explored and first settled by the English. It follows that the native people could be called Tsenacomacans. But to the English, the people they met along the banks of the rivers were variously called savages, salvages, naturals, natives, barbarians, heathens, or Indians. (Today most people, including modern descendants, refer to the Virginia Indians of Powhatan's chiefdom in Tidewater Virginia simply as Powhatans.) In the same way, the Powhatan River became the James River, named for King James I. In the eyes of many of the English, the land was vacant, the "savages" only another form of wildlife on the "untamed" landscape. In fact, the replacement of Tsenacomacan terms by English names was a first phase of the establishment of an English population to rule or replace the Tsenacomacans themselves. The king had claimed all of Tsenacomacah and beyond to the western sea and north to modern New Jersey, as long as no other "Christian" nations had any settlements there. To rename places with English names meant to the invaders—conquest.

The Tsenacomacans had their own names for themselves, their villages, their rivers, and even the new English arrivals, Tassantassas (King James and his people) (Figure 1.10). We can know this, ironically, only from English accounts, biased as these observations of a foreign culture are. Nonetheless, these depictions of Tsenacomacans provide a profile of a significant group of players in the Jamestown story, telling of a nation with a sophisticated language, customs, government, and economy.

The southernmost river in Tsenacomacah was the Powhatan (modern James River), named for the long-time native leader of the united chiefdom that greeted the English colonists in 1607. Who was he? Some speculate he was the cousin of Don Luis, who met the Jesuit settlers of the Chesapeake in 1570. It was Don Luis who went to Spain with the Jesuits and upon returning led a massacre of the missionaries. Whether or not the speculation is correct, Powhatan is almost invariably characterized by the English as the single most powerful chief among the Virginia Indians.

FIGURE 1.10   Altered John Smith's map of Virginia essentially delineates the bound-
aries of Powhatan's geographic influence, an area the Virginia Indians
called Tsenacomacah.

Source: The Library of Virginia.

Powhatan, also known as Wahunsonacock, was the head of a huge family
whose genealogy we can know in some measure[9] (Figure 1.11). A variety of records, mainly Smith's *Generall Historie* and Strachey's *Historie of Travell Into
Virginia Britania,* list the names of 30 of Powhatan's relatives and in-laws. Of
his three named brothers, the most can be known of Opechancanough, werow-
ance of the principal village on what the Tsenacomacans called the Pamunky River
(modern York River). Upon Powhatan's death in 1618, Opechancanough became
ruler either after or along with another brother, Opitchapam. Opechancanough led
two devastating assaults against the English in 1622 and 1644. When he was over
90 years old, he was assassinated at Jamestown, where he had been imprisoned
after the 1644 attacks on the English settlements.

One source claims Powhatan had "many more than one hundred" wives. The
names of at least a dozen of them are recorded. One wife, Oholasc, served as queen
of Quiyoughcohannock. The names of seven children of Powhatan's five sons and
two daughters are also on record. Three sons were werowances and the fourth,
Nantaquawis, was described by Captain John Smith as the "manliest, comliest and

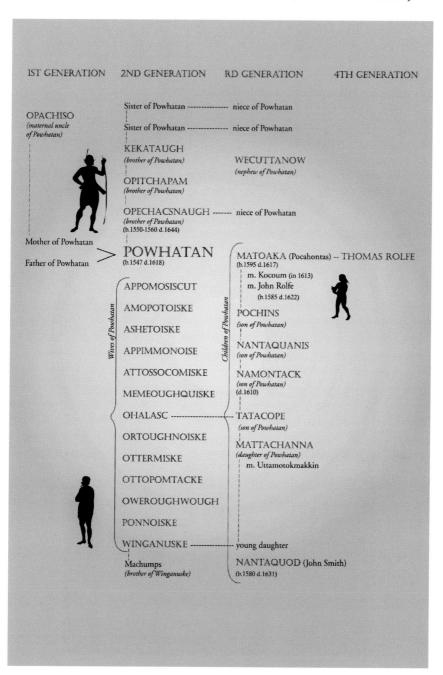

FIGURE 1.11 A hypothetical Powhatan family genealogical chart.

Source: Correll-Walls (Jamie May, JRF).

the boldest spirit I ever saw in a salvage." Matachanna, one of Powhatan's two daughters, married Uttamatomakkin (Tomocomo), a priest who traveled with her more famous sister, Pocahontas, and her English husband, John Rolfe, to England in 1616–1617. Tomocomo was not impressed with the land of the strange Tassantassas—but apparently Pocahontas was.

Pocahontas, the favored daughter of Powhatan who befriended John Smith, was kidnapped and proselytized by the English. She married John Rolfe in 1613, ushering in a period of peace between the settlers and the Indians. She also went to England, was received by the king, and shortly thereafter started for home. Lord Carew, in a letter to Sir Thomas Roe in 1616/1617, wrote that she waited "reluctantly" for favorable winds for her return voyage, sorely against her will. In the end, she died

FIGURE 1.12 Colorized engraving from life of Pocahontas made shortly before she died in England. She was buried at Gravesend, east of London, in 1617.

Source: Oil on tapestry, by Mary Ellen Howe, from an engraving by Simon de Passe, The Virginia Museum of History and Culture.

before sailing to Virginia. She is presumably buried in the chancel of St. George's Church, Gravesend, rebuilt after it burned in the early eighteenth century. Because of that fire and the rebuilding, Pocahontas's exact burial spot remains a challenging puzzle for archaeologists and interested direct descendants of the Jamestown colony.

Besides Uttamatomakkin and Pocahontas, a number of individual Tsenacomacans are recorded to have spent time with the English. Kemps, an Indian prisoner in the fort, taught the colonists to raise corn, and while he was a slave of George Percy, he guided the English during raids on the "Pasbeheans and the Chiconamians." Pepasschicher also guided the English. Mantiuas, also called Nantaquawis, a son of Powhatan, traveled with them, and Machumps was "sometyme in England." Powhatan had Amarice killed for staying in the fort without his permission.

It is a fact that Pocahontas married John Rolfe in 1614. Her first husband was an Indian named Kocoum. In asking permission from Sir Thomas Dale to marry Pocahontas, Rolfe seemed to be saying indirectly that such an intercultural marriage would be frowned upon by the English or at least be unusual. Other evidence suggests that intermarriage was officially scorned. Unofficially, however, there are strong reasons to suspect considerable mixing of the two cultures: the all-male population of the settlement during the first 16 months would have spurred such mixing; and in 1612 the Spanish reported that as many as "40 or 50 of the men had married with the salvages."

Despite the suggestion that Tsenacomacans had considerable access to the English and to Jamestown itself, serious animosity between the Indians and the English almost wiped the colony out during the "starving time" of 1609–1610. Some Virginia Indians besieged the fort that winter, and the siege was so effective that the Indians killed many of them if they ventured even short distances outside the fort and starvation and disease took a toll inside the fort walls. The Indians withheld even their occasional food deliveries. One explanation for the trouble may be the arrival at Jamestown of twenty women and children on the *Blessing* in the fall of 1609; perhaps the siege was a result of these newcomers' presence. It certainly must have sent a strong signal across Tsenacomacah that what might have been perceived as a small, perhaps temporary trading post was growing into something quite different: a permanent settlement of families. Extermination of the invaders may have appeared to be the only course of action.

Whatever the effect the immigration of women and children had on Tsenacomacan foreign policy, these newcomers certainly constitute another group of anonymous "diverse others" who influenced the developing "new England." We already know that the first English women, Mistress Forest and Anne Burras, came to the colony in the fall of 1608. They were not the only English women in town for long, however. According to the Spanish ambassador to England (and spy) Pedro de Zúñiga, one hundred women joined the four or five hundred men in the Gates 1609 flotilla to the colony. The ship *Blessing* brought 20 of these in 1609. Perhaps half the remaining 80 arrived as the remains of that fleet limped into the Jamestown port during the summer of 1609, and with the Bermuda ships *Deliverance* and *Patience* that arrived at Jamestown in May 1610. The names of the women who arrived on the *Blessing* are not known, but Temperance Flowerdew, wife of the future governor, Sir George Yeardley, came in 1609, as did Thomasine Cawsey, Elizabeth Joones, and Amtyte Waine, in time for them, along with the women from the *Blessing,* to experience the "starving" winter of 1609–1610. The list of named women grows to 35 by 1618, if the dates and the census of 1624–1625 are reliable. When Sir Thomas Gates returned to Virginia in 1611, he brought along his daughters, Margaret and Elizabeth. There must have been hundreds of anonymous "diverse other" women who braved the crossing and the "seasoning time" of a Virginia summer as well.

The siege of James Fort almost ended the colony. The two Bermuda-built ships that arrived in 1610 came not only with women but also with far too few provisions for a starving colony and the new arrivals. By June 1610, Gates decided to move the survivors out of Jamestown and set sail for England. Thanks to what has been characterized as last-second divine intervention, an advance vessel, followed by the arrival of Governor De La Warre and abundant fresh supplies, turned the

FIGURE 1.13 Artist's hypothetical rendering of Angela at Jamestown.

Source: Richard Schlecht, JRF.

deserters back to Jamestown in what seemed to be the nick of time. Upon his arrival in the James from Bermuda two months earlier, Gates had found 30 people with Percy at Point Comfort, literally healthy as clams, living off the seafood there. De La Warre's timely June arrival in 1610 assured Jamestown would live on to become the first enduring English colony in North America.

Until 1699, Jamestown was the capitol of the colony but it never became the heavily populated city the Crown and various Governors wanted it to be. The Virginia census taken in 1624 lists only 124 people living within the bounds of what had become known as James Citty: 115 immigrants and nine enslaved "negroes."[10] The Jamestown African population began in 1619, when a woman named Angela arrived on the English privateer ship, the *Treasurer.* Captain William Pierce, a prominent Jamestown merchant and tobacco planter, bought Angela "Angelo, a negro woman" who lived at the Pierce household, while "five negro women and three negro men" were the Jamestown servants of Sir George Yeardley. There is little other demographic data about the seventeenth-century population of Jamestown since the official records of James City County were destroyed during the Civil War. But we can have hints of the aggregate Virginia population. In 1622, about 1388 people lived in the colony when the Virginia Indians attached and killed 347. Another count by an English investigative Royal Commission reviewing the state of the colony in 1676–1677 reported a total Virginia population of 40,000, 32,000 immigrants and native born, 6000 indentured servants, and 2000 slaves.[11] By the end of the next century, Virginia had a population of 10,000 slaves.[12] Certainly, almost all the Virginia black population labored on the large plantation tobacco fields of the *nouveau riche*.[13] The African-American seventeenth-century Jamestown population is unknown after the 1624 muster but it is likely that their numbers grew exponentially until the Virginia government was moved to Williamsburg by 1699. Evidence of these anonymous enslaved people who occupied the seventeenth-century Jamestown houses, walked the streets, tended to the gardens, loaded the merchant ships, and probably left some archaeological imprint on the seventeenth-century Jamestown landscape, at this writing, remains virtually unseen.

Notes

1 David Quinn, ed. *Observations Gathered Out of "Discourse of the Plantation of the Southern Colony by the English,1606 written by the Honorable George Percy"* (Charlottesville, VA, 1967), 15.

2 John Smith. *The Complete Works of Captain John Smith, 1580–1631*, Philip Barbour (London, 1986), 2: 225.

3 Louis Wright. *Two Narratives, "William Strachey a True Reportory"* (Charlottesville, VA, 1964), 63–64,

4 Edward Haile. Jamestown Narratives, "Don Diego de Molina. May, 1613" (Champlain, VA, 1998), 749.

5 Gravenhage Colectie Leupe, Algemeenrijkarchief, The Hague, Velh 619.89. Michael Jarvis and Jeroen van Driel brought this map to my attention.

6 Strachey, in Wright, *Voyage to Virginia*, 79–82.

7 Catherine Correll-Walls. Jamestown Biographies Data Base Project, Jamestown Rediscovery Achieves.

8 Haile. A History of Travel. 613.

9 Catherine Correll-Walls. Jamestown Rediscovery research files (Jamestown, VA).

10 John Frederick Dorman. *Adventurers of Purse and Person, Musters of the Inhabitants in Virginia 1624/25*, First Families of Virginia (Richmond, VA, 1987), 29–34.

11 John Davenport Neville. *Bacon's Rebellion Abstracts of Materials in the Public Records Project* (Jamestown Foundation, ND), 267.

12 Edmund S. Morgan. *American Slavery, American Freedom* (New York, 1975), 108–130.

13 John Coombes. *Feeding the "Machine" The Development of Slavery and Slave Society in Colonial Virginia*, Dissertation College of William and Mary, 15396223434 passim.

2

CONTRIVED AND REDUCED

In September 1996 at a well-attended Jamestown press conference, Virginia Governor George Allen enthusiastically proclaimed "We have found the 1607 James Fort." He went on to declare the day "James Fort Day" which would officially go on the State of Virginia's calendar to commemorate the site of the Fort at *Historic Jamestowne*. Allen also said that the day would remain on the calendar until July 30, 2019, the 400th anniversary of the meeting of the first representative governmental assembly in North America. He explained that as Virginia would recognize the founding of the Fort in 2007 there was also a need to commemorate that assembly meeting which was so prophetic, sowing the seeds of what would become the structure of the Government of the United States.

Finding archaeological signs of the Fort during the first two years of the Jamestown Rediscovery Project, 1994–1996 began to dispel the 150-year belief that the fort site had been erased by James River shoreline erosion. For example, the most prominent Jamestown historians wrote the following discouraging words:

The greater part of the ground enclosed by the triangular fort has been destroyed by the abrasion of the Island bank[1]

In all probability, it [the fort] stood on ground that has been washed into the James River.[2]

(8)Archaeological evidence can prove nothing [about James Fort], for the undoubted site has been washed into the James River ... .[3]

Actually, while discovery of the remains of what appeared to be parts of 1607 James Fort began to cast doubt on that "lost" legend, it took another nine years to literally connect all the buried dots (log wall impressions) and dashes (the wall

DOI: 10.4324/9781003441670-2

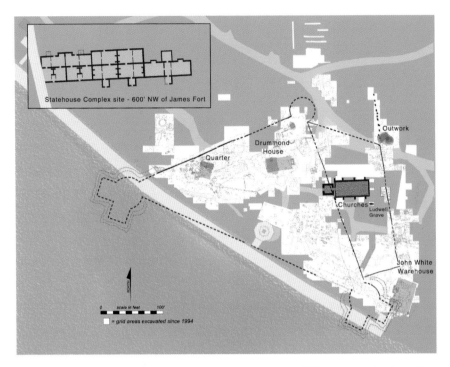

FIGURE 2.1   Location map of Jamestown's Archaeological "Remains to be Seen," the Fort as first "contrived" and soon "reduced" (dotted red line). Outwork, John White Warehouse, the Drummond House, the Quarter, Ludwell grave, the Churches 1617–1907, and the Statehouse Complex.

Source: Jamie May, JRF.

trenches) that made up the complete triangular shape it was reported to be. Finally, we could say emphatically, yes, 1607 James Fort lived on! The lines we found measured within a few feet of Secretary William Strachey's 1610 measurements of the one-acre three-walled enclosure. James Fort was found beyond a reasonable doubt, a rare instant when archaeological and historical evidence can lead to a conclusion that is undeniable.[4]

But to confuse matters, a document suggested that the triangular fortification was not all there was to find. Again in 1608, Captain John Smith wrote that the Fort was "reduced to a five square form." The question arose, "what could that mean?" Who designed and who allegedly transformed the triangular into a pentagon? Certainly not the men Smith found when he returned to the Fort from a reconnaissance trip up river in September 1607. At that time, he indicated that the town was in complete decay and the people "all sick, the rest some lame, some bruised—all unable to do anything but complain ... many dead, the harvest rotting and nothing done." It was clear that the Fort needed serious revitalization at that point and that would take new leadership to do it. In September, the council elected Smith president. It seems apparent that under his direction further construction and a redesign of the Fort were carried out. He went on to write more fort design detail: [It was]

> environed with a Palizados of fourteen or fifteen feet, and each as much as three or four men could carrie … we had three Bulwarks, foure and twentie peece of ordinance upon convenient plat-forms … [the overall plan] reduced to the form of this (…) [figure omitted but later called five-square].[5]

But before the apparent reconfiguration, who came up with the original triangular design? Smith hints at an answer: [the leaders] "Councilors contrived" it. This in all probability must have meant that some of the elected leaders designed and directed the construction. That made sense since all of the first council was made up of military men holding the rank of *Captain*: Master [Captain] Edward Maria Wingfield, Bartholomew Gosnold, Christopher Newport, John Martin, John Ratcliffe, George Kendall, and John Smith. This, we can conclude meant they all were experienced military men who, in England or in foreign wars, had once led either a hundred-man Company or a ship full of mariners.[6] Another Captain Gabriel Archer must have joined them and contributed New World experience to the contrivers. At first, the Fort was no more than a flimsy "wall" of tree branches fashioned by Captain Kendall. But after a major Indian attack, a triangular enclosure made of palisades (upright side-by-side log walls) was raised in June–July 1607. Much of that construction time Smith was away on an exploration trip up river so we can conclude that the other experienced military men and President of the Council, Wingfield, lead the construction.

Given that we now know the archaeologically defined footprint of the Fort, it is clear what the "contrivers" contrived. With that new knowledge, we can learn how much they knew about fort building. That in turn reflects upon the wisdom of the Virginia Company leaders. They must have had some understanding of the danger the 100 plus Jamestown settlers would face in Virginia when they sent the Captains off to Virginia and thus enlisted the experienced Wingfield, Gosnold, and Archer. And what they designed and directed the men to build in a short 19-day effort is indeed clear evidence of their military leadership experience.

It was the 57-year-old President of the Council, Captain Edward Maria Wingfield, who was most familiar with Elizabethan Period fort design. Decades before he landed at Jamestown, he was a soldier for some years in Ireland and, significantly, a Captain of a Company of Foot supporting the Dutch Republican Army who fought against the Spanish in a fierce battle at Zutphin in 1586. A detailed sixteenth-century map of Zutphin shows fortifications on an island in front of the town and on the south bank of the Ijssel River (Figure 2.2). The English besieged the town and captured part of the town's fortifications and presumably Captain Wingfield participated. According to a contemporary map, that fort design included

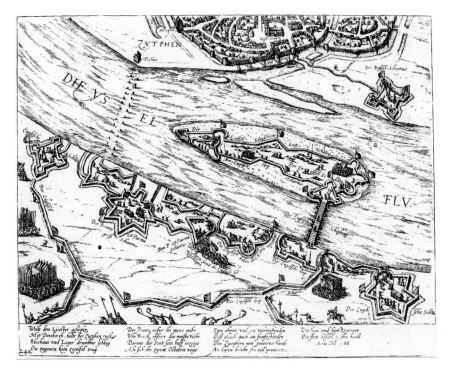

FIGURE 2.2   Forts at the siege of Zutphen in the Netherlands 1586, where, in the vicinity, Edward Maria Wingfield fought the Spanish. Note triangular fort with extensions.

triangular inner enclosures with corner bastions. It follows then that probably Wingfield had firsthand knowledge of how effective that design could be in battle. He also apparently performed there well under fire for he and his brother were noted in an Army Roll of 1589 as *"captains of success"* and one record indicates he was eventually knighted for his service there.[7] So considering Wingfield's stellar military background as a Captain in the Dutch War, it made perfect sense for him to draw on his firsthand knowledge of triangular fort designs. He would know that a fort with three walls could go up faster than the usual four and still be secure. Speed was, of course, of the essence at Jamestown as the builders were constantly under fire from Virginia Indians during construction. But the English/Dutch Zutphin defense system was more than triangular enclosures. So it is little wonder that more of our archaeological evidence revealed that James Fort quickly evolved beyond its first-built triangular design.

Other leaders had fort-building experience. In May–June 1607, when the James Fort was "contrived" Captain Gosnold already had firsthand knowledge of building a New World defense. Five years before he led an expedition of a short-lived English settlement on Cuttyhunk Island, one of the Elizabeth Isles near Martha's

Vineyard. After exploring Cape Cod and the islands to the south, Gosnold's colonizing group chose the Island for their settlement mainly because it had an inner lake surrounding a smaller island, a naturally "moated" defendable place. There he built a "fort." In this case, it was apparently only a timber building, perhaps a blockhouse that would serve as a safe haven for his 20 fellow settlers even without a surrounding palisade. Also Gosnold had Captain Gabriel Archer with him to keep a daily journal describing the settlement. So Archer too may had a hand in the design of the Cuttyhunk "Fort" which, like James Fort, went up in 19 days.[8] Although he was not a councilor like Wingfield and Gosnold, it makes sense that Archer's fort building experience at Cuttyhunk in New England probably also contributed to the design and construction of the Jamestown Fort. So one can conclude that all three James Fort designers were hardly inexperienced amateurs. But they were not engineers. They did not need to be.

Remember the Virginia Company officials knew that the Spanish were strongly opposed to any English New World colonization. Consequently, as protection from a probable Spanish reprisal, the Company instructed the colonists to go 100 leagues up a major river to establish the settlement where the river banks narrowed enough for them to be able to fire on Spanish ships from both banks. And in fact, the Company had advised the would-be colonists NOT to build a fort at all because the Virginia Indians would see this a sign of invasion. But within 10 days of the landing at Jamestown, a major native attack at Jamestown made it obvious that the Indians and not the Spanish were the actual clear and present danger. So within a month, the settlers enclosed Jamestown with the triangular palisaded Fort even as they were under fire. And the settlers realized what they needed was a defense against both enemies as their military manual outlined: "... *two sorts of ffortefycacons, one for the induringe of assaults and Battery* [the Spanish, and] ... *the other* [fort needs to be in] *some place of Advantage, and there to make some Pallysadoes ...* " [for protection from the Indians]. But in reality, the leaders had to opt for the wooden palisade fort on high ground as soon as they could. Consequently, James Fort was not well designed to withstand Spanish ship cannons. As it turned out it never had to be; "[only] ... *sufficiency strong for these savages.*"[9]

However, one of the military manuals of the era advises "In the delineation of a fort that shall serve for a royall frontier, the figure triangle is not to be used ..." Yet the manual goes on to qualify that advice, stating a triangle could be used "... *on those watrie grounds where it cannot be* [easily] *approached.*"[10] So the choice of the highest ground facing the James River on Jamestown Island especially within the marshes that surrounded it indeed qualified as a good place to speedily build a triangular defense. Further, the manual advises fort builders:

Where water may be founde, the fort ... needth not dig the ditches so deep as in dry ground, for it will be free from surpise, skale and mining ... Moreover the fort standing neare unto any river, may receive great commodities of it for the bringing of things necessarie unto it, for... the maintaining of it, ... (p. 3).[11]

No wonder the shallow dry moat we found archaeologically along the surviving circle of the east bulwark did not have to be deep to be effective. By the same token, there was no point for the builders to trench along the walls. That lack of encircling moats also indicates Wingfield was familiar with the fortification manual. Further, there was no point in building angle-sided bastions so commonly found in European star-shaped forts which were designed for deflecting cannon fire and for eliminating unprotected "dead" zones, which was a major problem with archaic round bastion designs.

There is also strong archaeological evidence of Smith's five-sided "new design" or at least the beginnings of it. We already knew that very early in our fort archaeological excavation, an additional palisade wall trench existed beginning at the point where the circular east bastion joined the main fort bastion wall. This line made a right angle with the Fort wall and extended 60 feet to a post-in-the-ground "factory" building site. We also knew that another small section of palisade extended east at a 45-degree angle from the point where the circular north bastion joined the main fort bastion wall. Those discoveries appeared to be suggesting that the palisaded James Fort design extended to the east. But these clues were not pursued archaeologically at that time of discovery because it became clear that the original triangular fort, the focus of our Jamestown Rediscovery Project from the beginning, lay to the west. Excavations concentrated on remnants of those walls and the Fort interior for the next 20 years.[12]

As we already know, archeological digging progressed during the early 2000s by "following" the west palisade wall which revealed the complete triangular form. It also became obvious that the overall main fort design was not just "a triangle" but an isosceles triangle. This "discovery" in the field seemed like great insight. But then it occurred to us that the fort dimensions given by William Strachey in 1610 included two sides of equal length (100 yards each) which meant that the fort *had* to be an isosceles triangle. And the fact that the third side along the river was (120 yards) made for simple angles, basically a right angle (90 degrees) on the north and 45-degree angles on the two "corners" at the riverside. That being the case, the Wingfield *et.al* triangular design would have been simple to lay out on the ground. Its very simplicity was also in keeping with fortification manuals. According to one, no special equipment was needed to form the ground plan; the lines of a bulwark and presumably the walls (curtains) of a fort were to be established by using "stakes, lines (ropes?) and paces."

> to the practice of delineation [of a bulwarke or fort] ... set down a stake and stretch a line betwirt stake and stake, and with a spade make a little cut alongst the line.[distance measured by] paces at five foote every pace.[13]

Even though the Fort shape was a simple isolate triangle that doesn't mean there were no challenges in actually laying out the enclosure wall lines on the virgin ground. These can be understood with a certain amount of fact-grounded

FIGURE 2.3   Artist's conception of the settlers building James Fort.

Source: Sidney King (United States Geological Survey, USGS).

imagination. I can envision the men performing simple geometry: First, they must have paced out two equal palisade lines. From that point, according to the manual instructions, all that was needed to lay out the full James Fort triangle was to simply stake out lines in this case two 300 foot long and connect them with a line 460 feet (120 yards) long. This was the isosceles triangle that produced two 45-degree angles on the south and a right angle on the third "corner" to the north. Then palisades were anchored in the ground along the three lines and "where the lines met" the builders added bulwarks. There is also reason to conclude that these circular bulwarks were even more elementary to lay out on the ground than the three walls. All the men had to do was to stake a rope where the side wall lines met, stretch the rope out to the length of the diameter of the intended bulwark, and then simply inscribe a line by encircling the stake at rope's length. Palisades would be planted along the circle line where it intersected the two nearest walls, creating a circular bulwark. Easy enough (Figure 2.4).

The archaeological evidence of these bulwark circles indicated that they were intended to be about 50 feet in diameter. There was even more logic than that involved. Since the south corners formed the 45-degree angles, the two south bastions wound up having a greater firing range (215 degrees) and then the north bulwark (170 degrees). This made sense militarily since the threat had already proven to be the Indians on land and not likely the Spanish ships approaching on the main river. And apparently the round north bulwark was considered to be enough to repel

FIGURE 2.4   The north bulwark palisade trench and seating posthole for the James Fort
flag pole/watchtower.

Source: Michael Lavin, JRF.

an Indian attack from the marsh. All this staking, pacing, trenching, and palisade
construction turned out to enclose about one acre of land, apparently a space considered to be enough to protect the 100+ settlers inside (a basic Company of Foot).
Again according to the manual, the construction of dry moats along the walls and
bastions was seemingly unnecessary. Nonetheless, we found moats at both river
front bulwarks. Actually, creating the triangular-shaped fort was indeed mathemati-
cally simple. That was a good thing. Remember the men were under attack the
whole time it took to secure the one-acre structure.

The simple ground plan layout was the least of the Fort building challenges for
the "contrivers." The actual construction of all the walls required a herculean excavation effort, digging over 1450' of trenches 2 1/2' deep and felling, carrying, and
planting over 700 logs. In the summer heat this, of course, was seriously stressful
on the 40 workers left in camp, so much so that Smith wrote that this exertion in
the summer heat was one cause of the rash of deaths among the men. That occurred
just after the Fort was completed (July 15).

Based on 1607–1608 Tyndall's and Zuniga's maps and archaeological evidence,
it is clear that the Wingfield/Gosnold simple triangle design with three round bastions was only the 1607 version of the Fort. The next year the Zuniga map indicates
the addition of squared corner projections on the two river front bastions. This design change was more attuned to fighting off direct cannon attacks on the river side

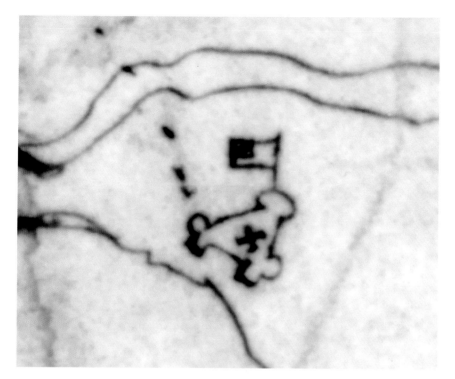

FIGURE 2.5 Zuniga Map of James Fort 1608.

Source: The British Library.

of the Fort. So despite the reality of Indian attacks coming from across the Back River and marshes, apparently the men did not rule out the threat of an attack from Spanish ships. This could well be a *part* of Smith's alterations (Figure 2.5).

But while it sounds like Smith and his men rebuilt the entire original triangular Fort with taller upright log palisades in 1608, there is no archaeological sign of it. The wall trenches on the south and west only show the imprint of a single undisturbed line of the decayed upright logs. The east wall is a different archaeological story. That wall trench shows signs that it had been dismantled probably in 1610 by physically digging around each log and pulling them out without inserting new ones. So Smith probably was referring to an *expansion* of the original triangular palisade wall converting it into that reportedly five-sided pentagon. This may have been the full Wingfield plan from the start. That would have been more like the evolving elaborate plan of the various enclosed forts he saw and probably helped build at Zutphin. Considering the two angles of the additional palisaded walls, 90 degrees on the south and 45 degrees on the north, it seems that Wingfield may have planned to actually double the original triangle forming an overall diamond shape. This would have been not unlike the palisaded fort raised in New England at

FIGURE 2.6 Aerial view of reconstructed Plymouth Fort.

Source: J. Eric Deetz, University of Illinois, Urbana.

Plymouth in 1620 (Figure 2.6). Nonetheless, owing to Wingfield's political problems and the great starvation at Jamestown in the summer of 1607, his greater
design could not be implemented before he was deposed as President and sent back
to England.

If there was indeed a *greater* Wingfield design, then apparently Smith knew
about it. With Wingfield gone, Smith's revived men got back to Fort construction
in the Spring of 1608 which included the aforementioned redesign of the two river
side bulwarks plus the addition secured space that was partially enclosed on the
north and south by extended palisades.

The northernmost extended line ended next to a single sizeable posthole
(Figure 2.7–2.9). The posthole discovery turned out to be more exciting than it
sounds. It was also the terminus of a faint and shallow palisade trench leading
south where it connected to the "factory" building that we had found early in the
Jamestown Rediscovery Project excavations. These two palisade lines enclosed
an additional half acre of Fort land. Attached to the one-acre main triangle, it did
form Smith's "five-sided" Fort. This add-on space was a long and narrow part of
a logical re-design. The factory building had been found to have a cellar near the
river shore which included a partially below-ground musketeer's shot platform
along the east side. With the extension palisade line in place, this defensive position created an additional outwork/bulwark.

Breaks in the northern palisade trench revealed how the men could move in and
out of the secured area. Two 2′-wide gaps were found along the line and a final
gap was found near that major posthole location. This seems to be an overlapping
"gap gate" which was apparently designed to allow for protected movement in and
out of the extension compound between the two curved overlapping walls. This
created what was known in military terms as a sallyport, a secure and controlled
entryway into a fort. A similar sallyport was apparently used in one of the English forts at Zutphin which re-enforces the idea that it was Wingfield's unfinished

FIGURE 2.7   The 1608 Fort palisade trench marking the north wall of the Smith's "reduction."

Source: Michael Lavin, JRF.

FIGURE 2.8 Artist's conception of a reconstructed James Fort showing the 1608–1610 eastern 1/2 acre "reduction."

Source: Jamie May, JRF.

design carried on by Smith. But this was not the only outwork in that Wingfield/ Smith design.

The single palisade post not only marked a corner of the extension but it appeared to be the southwest corner of an adjacent defensive outwork cellar. Postholes along the clay cellar walls indicated where upright timbers once supported the outwork superstructure, which was built at an angle to the extension corner. Like the factory, this building's position could provide a clear range of fire to protect the extension walls in both directions. In a simplified form, this design element also mimics some of the Zutphen outworks and the more formal defensive works known as sconces. This again appears to be further evidence of Wingfield's greater plan that Smith likely carried forward.

Support postholes along the cellar walls indicated that after the men dug the cellar, slots in the walls had to be cut above the postholes in the floor ostensibly to support premeasured timbers of the superstructure framing. At least that could account for the slots which do not appear to have been made to stabilize the posts. We also found an extremely large and deep posthole containing cobbles at the bottom in the center of what appeared to be a main room. This suggests it supported the greatest weight of the superstructure perhaps beneath a heavy cannon or a blockhouse pyramidal roof.

But unlike the factory to the south, the builders of the outwork attempted to put in a square timber-lined well in the cellar. Defensively it made sense to include a well *inside* the protected outwork area structure which would make the building capable of withstanding a siege. But our excavation of the well shaft below the 10′-deep water table encountered a sub-strata so sandy and unstable that we could not continue the excavation. Even our own wooden casing and a mechanical pump

FIGURE 2.9   Overhead view of the soil evidence of the northern and southern extended
Fort palisade trenches terminating at a single structural posthole and the
aborted square well (JRF Danny Schmidt).

could not keep ahead of the in-rushing water and silt. These unstable shaft walls
and a lack of artifacts in the fill strongly suggested that the original builders also
had to give up sinking the well shaft before they too could shore it up. So despite
the fact that installing a well inside a defensive building was a good idea in theory,
in practice it turned out to be an impossible scheme.

Occupation levels on the cellar floor indicated that the easternmost room had
been constructed first and used even when ground water or seepage into the superstructure brought in silt (Figure 2.10). Apparently, to remedy the problem of

FIGURE 2.10   Outwork cellar rooms during excavation showing natural sand floors in
the two cellar rooms and the main cobbled support post location (arrow).

Source: Michael Lavin, JRF.

a muddy floor, sand was brought in to raise the walking surface—which covered
the aborted well hole. The added sand apparently did not completely get rid of the
mud problem so some timbers were laid here and there on the mired floor to form a
more stable but interrupted walking surface. Mud was not a problem in the addition
(room B); builders wisely built that floor level above the seepage zone.

As usual, this James Fort cellar had some occupation deposit on the floor. Very
few artifacts were found in that fill, but nonetheless they were objects one would
expect to find left from the occasional use of the rooms by the soldiers. For example, at one point in time, some of the men apparently ate in Room B leaving a
concentration of discarded pig and bird bones.

There were very few artifacts in the occupation level which suggests that the
men only manned outwork periodically. The same was true for the occupation floor
in the factory cellar. However, above the working floors, we found multiple layers
of garbage and trash thrown into both of the abandoned cellar holes. But the outwork debris was markedly different. As we have seen, the factory and many other
abandoned cellars found in the Fort were almost certainly filled all at once with
garbage and trash that had accumulated from 1607 to the 1609–1610, the starving
time years. But unlike most of those earlier backfilled cellars, when abandoned
washed-in silt containing few artifacts filled the outwork cellar. This must indicate
that the cellar stood vacant until it was slowly filled in sometime after 1630, the

FIGURE 2.11   Cross-section, lower cellar fill layers: occupation, bottom, fallen mud wall, lower left, and washed-in silt, garbage, and trash above all.

Source: Michael Lavin, JRF.

earliest manufacture date of a fragment of pottery in that layer. However, it is possible that the outwork building lasted longer than the aforementioned factory structure because it was still useful as an outwork to protect an ultimate greater fortified area. And there is some archaeological and documentary evidence that there was indeed a greater fortified area.

In 1611, Ralph Hamor wrote: "The town itself ... is reduced into a handsome form ... [and it] hath been lately and newly and strongly *impaled* ... ."[14] A "paling" was not a palisade but rather a very substantial fence, high and strong enough to effectively protect a town from assault. It would require sturdy posts in the ground spanned by two or more rails that would support upright side-by-side thick clapboards (pales). As archaeologists have found time and time again, a structure built this way would leave a line of evenly spaced large and deep posthole soil marks with smaller dark patches of soil in them where the post had rotten away (a postmold). That is what we found leading away from the outwork.

Indeed, we found two intersecting lines of oversized and holes with varied depth extending north from the outwork (Figure 2.12). The lines overlapped indicating that one line cut into and therefore post-dated it. This superimposition likely indicated that one line stood long enough to need a replacement. The holes were regularly spaced 9 feet apart except at a point halfway along the line where two postholes were 4′ apart indicating the location of a gateway.

FIGURE 2.12 Lines of "paling" posts leading north (top) from the outwork cellar.
Source: Danny Schmidt, JRF.

Excavation of the posthole fill revealed diminishing depth from deep at the outwork then incrementally shallower and shallower as the line extended to the north until it disappeared altogether. The diminishing and retreating depth proves that the ground had been increasingly shaved down to the north after the paling ceased to exist. This was probably done either by the Confederate soldiers and slaves during the construction of the nearby Civil War earthwork in 1861 or by APVA workmen to gather fill for enhancing the 1907 reconstructed church yard. Only one artifact, a non-descript and un-datable iron object, was found in all the soil deposited in the paling support postholes. That almost utter absence of artifacts was telling. As we have seen, the lack of artifacts in deposits has proven to be a sign that they dated to the very early years of the English occupation. In other words, when these paling posts were planted, not enough time passed for the settlers to lose enough of anything that would inadvertently wind up in the paling postholes during their construction. In this case, we could get away with ignoring the archaeological rule "that absence of evidence is not evidence of absence" since so many James Fort deposits devoid of artifacts proved to be from the first few years of the English occupation. Actually, many of these completely barren features could be dated by written references or their comparative stratigraphic context.[15]

At any rate, finding that these postholes dated from the earliest years of Jamestown occupation is good reason to suggest that the two posthole lines are in fact postholes created to construct Hamor's 1611 paling. And even though the paling lines were gradually graded away, logic would suggest that the barrier continued on, crossing the "pitch and tar swamp" to the north and on across to Back Creek. There the defense line may have connected to the blockhouse that stood on the banks of Back Creek. At that point, the line likely turned west to connect to another blockhouse located at the eastern end of the Island isthmus, in order

… to stop the disorders of our disorderly thieves and the savages [at the]… blockhouse in the neck of our isle", "… [it] kept at a garrison to entertain the savages' trade and none to pass nor repass-savage nor Christian without the president's order".[16] "… there are also without this town in the island … two blockhouses to observe and watch lest the Indians at any time should swim over the Back River and come into the island.[17]

It is difficult to see how the enlarged paling connecting James Fort and the two blockhouses along on the north side of the Island could repel any attack. But added to the paling on the east and north, Back Creek and the James River would naturally complete the barrier. At any rate, how much of the area between the Fort and the blockhouses was protected by a paling is an open question for future archaeology to answer even though, as we will see (FT NT), "blockhouse hill" has almost certainly eroded into the James. The strata of the outwork cellar was no exception.

There is little doubt that the outwork was a contemporary part of a greater Jamestown defense system. How so? First of all, analysis of many deposits of cellar fill has continually proven to reveal an evolving Fort in remarkable detail. Our usual care in reading and then removing this strata in cellars indeed revealed soil layer sequences deposited during events that happened when the cellar was in use, ca. 1608–1610, and after the building was abandoned (1630).

The layer cake sequence of infill began with that aforementioned accumulation of butchered animal bones on the original clay floor, including chicken, goose, turkey, and pig. This deposit was like a time-capsule obviously suggesting that during one day in the life of the outwork, sentries gathered in the cellar for a well-stocked meal. Then as time passed, stratigraphic soil continued to accumulate after the meal. On top of the bone level in places along the walls, we next uncovered a deposit of a variegated colored clay, a mixture identical to deposits found above other occupation layers in every cellar in the Fort. This was almost certainly residue from collapsed mud walls. Here the deposit was not as widespread and voluminous as we found in other cellars suggesting that, unlike the other Fort buildings, clay covered walls were only a minor part of the outwork building. After all, an outwork blockhouse needed to be made of solid timber, so flimsy mud walls could have to be only a minor part of this serious defensive building. In any event, the presence

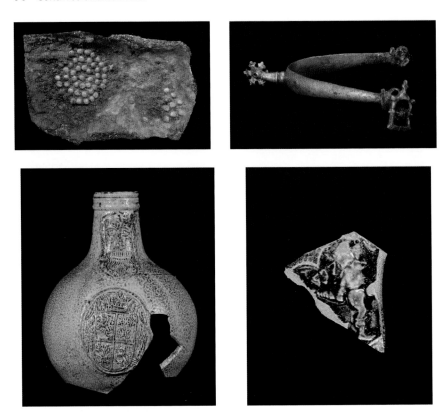

FIGURE 2.13   Selected artifacts found in refuse layers of the outwork cellar fill: (Left to right) an embossed box lid, a brass spur, a Bartman jug, and fragment of a stoneware "Peasant's Wedding" jug dated 1597.

Source: Charles Durfor, JRF.

of collapsed earthen wall material must be evidence that the above superstructure of the outwork was down when that mud wall layer accumulated. Datable artifacts thrown into the abandoned cellar hole thereafter establish the date of the major back-filling of the cellar hole (Figure 2.13).

Above the mixed wall clay, the layers of that sandy fill were found contained artifacts suggesting it accumulated after about 1630. Then resting on top of the sand, many dark silty "wax-like" levels accumulated leaving little doubt that the hole was left open to the elements for a time resulting in a deposit of more eroded clay. But occasional artifacts and an unusual waxy-like soil suggested there were periods when the colonists discarded brush and occasionally inadvertently some trash over an extended period of time.

But below all that, we also found metal from recycled armor just above the cellar occupation soil zone. This was puzzling. Why cut up armor for reuse and why throw the leftover metal into the open cellar hole? One explanation could be that finding these fragmented artifacts is probably another case of the English adapting to the reality of Indian guerilla warfare. They were simply cutting up useless body armor into small metal plates to make more flexible scaled "jacks of plate."[18] Nonetheless, the dates of the artifacts from the waxy deposit are consistently datable to the first third of the seventeenth century. And some of the fragmented pottery found in sandy fill and in the more organic soil above it suggests the fact that it all had come from a common trash deposit in the Fort then dumped into the cellar in a short period of time. For instance, a number of other fragments of a dated (1597) sherd of a German stoneware jug found in the "waxy" cellar fill were recovered in interior Fort deposits. Here is a case where two contextual deposits of the same broken object indicate past related events, someone breaking and depositing an original broken vessel in the Fort and then someone borrowing that fill from the Fort to fill in an abandoned cellar hole. In any event, the final fill in the cellar hole suggests that the outwork had a rather "un-ceremonious" end. Finally, as it became nothing more than a depression it became a dumping ground for brick-and-mortar waste from construction of the Brick Church nearby.

South of the blockhouse cellar, a single outsized and deep posthole and post mold was found. We assumed that this post was one of many that had been planted to support another major Fort building so we extended excavations in all directions looking for more. That effort came up empty. Consequently, the purpose of this single enormous post was puzzling, but that hole was not a one-off find. Another single oversized and deep posthole was found early in the Fort excavations at the point where the Fort palisade trench began to curve to form the north bulwark (Figure 2.4). It seemed that that hole was put in that position to support a flagpole. But now we had two lone large posts that were at strategic points in the fortification plan suggesting that they served a similar defensive purpose.

Solving the mystery led us to a review of seventeenth-century Fort drawings collected by the Dutch cartographer, Vingboons[19] (Figures 2.14 and 2.15). He compiled and published an astonishing collection of them indicating that they had been located at major trading cities around the globe (1600–1637).

Some of these illustrations showed tall single posts at the bastions. The posts appear to have ladder "steps" so they appear to be like ship's "crows' nests" which offered a better view of the surrounding land and sea. Vingboons also shows other examples of the single poles of a different sort. Some have raised iron fire cages on top that at night could be used as signal towers or "light houses" (beacons) to guide ships or to send signals at night. One Fort drawing seems to show that these could be both watchtowers and flagpoles. If that were the case, the detail of the contemporary description of James Fort makes more sense.

"... *at every angle or corner [of the Fort] a bulwarke or a watch tower is raised...*"[20] This must have meant the two postholes were supports for the watch towers. So the one posthole base found in the Fort could have been used for both a lookout and a flag pole and the other near our Fort outwork used for a lookout

FIGURE 2.14   Flag pole/watch tower in Fort Elmina, West Africa.

FIGURE 2.15   Ladder watch tower in Fort Keulen bulwark, Brazil.

and/or a beacon. In that case, it seems Strachey's description should have read: "a bulwarke AND a watch tower."

But probably more significant than being a defensive outwork, there appeared to be another reason for the eastern Fort "reduction" palisade, produce gardens. As every gardener knows, there is a vital need to fence gardens from ever ravenous native animals. The first settlers seemed to be well aware of this from day one. They made gardens *"May 13, 1607 '... now falleth every man to work ... some make gardens. June 15, 1607' we also sown most of our corn ... It sprang a man's height from the ground."*[21] Most historians believe that the cause of so many deaths in the first summer among the settlers was starvation partially caused by the fact that they arrived too late in the year to plant while wasted precious planting time prospecting for gold. So the reference to the great height of the corn in only a month has always been dismissed as merely exaggeration in order to assure Company investors that the colonists were hard at work making Jamestown self-sustaining. But our excavations give solid archaeological evidence that the colonists did plant and in fact established enclosed gardens.

Removal of early twentieth-century APVA landscaping fill in the Fort extension area demonstrated that crops were planted as early as 1607 and that they were productive until at least 1609. We found extensive patterns of garden ditches parallel to the east Fort wall (Figure 2.16). They were almost certainly dug to create

FIGURE 2.16   1607 planting furrows (dark inter-furrow ditches) within the Fort extension.
Source: Danny Schmidt, JRF.

planting rows by "stacking" the dugout topsoil on the natural topsoil between them. In the early years of our excavations, another series of these ditches were found extending at a right angle from the orientation of the east Fort wall. At the time, we did not realize they were evidence of gardening. They were just considered "puzzling." But our later excavations showed a distinct pattern of a number of these soil "streaks" east of the Fort and in the Fort extension. We now realize that the ditches are evidence of gardening and once more we able to date them by "reading" the soil stains in light of written records. Significantly, the 1608 "reduced" palisade trench occasionally cut through some of the planting rows proving the rows predated the palisade. So it follows that the planting rows do likely date to the "gardens" recorded on May 13, 1607. Also there is every reason to conclude that some of the rows were re-used perhaps furnishing the corn crops that those ill-provisioned immigrants wiped out in a month.[22] So as much as the extension palisade may have been successful keeping poaching animals out, they could not protect the crops from the ravenous newcomers. At any rate, the garden planting row discovery is a good example of archaeology contributing significant new insight into the Jamestown story. The standard condemnation of "lazy" gentlemen failing to produce their own food seems to be an over-generalization. The archaeological evidence proves that at least some among the troops and probably even some of the gentlemen knew the basics of husbandry. There is no doubt that John Smith did. He came from a farming family in Lincolnshire.

FIGURE 2.17   Eighteenth-century horse skeleton found in a churchyard boundary ditch.
Source: Danny Schmidt, JRF.

James Fort Trojan House?

In June of 2013 while seeking to define more of the Fort extension and its planting furrows, we quite unexpectedly uncovered an articulated horse skeleton. It lay buried in a ditch that seemed to be marking the northern boundary of both the planting rows and the later churchyard burial ground. We knew that documents fail to mention details about horses except that six horses and a mare were sent to the colony in 1609. We wondered if this was one of them and if so, the possibility that this discovery might add more detail about the immigrating animals besides their number. Not so. While our meticulous excavation revealed the almost complete horse skeleton, dramatically looking like it died in stride, it turned out that it this horse died in the later eighteenth century. Directly underneath the skeleton, we found a button known to have been manufactured after ca. 1760.

Nonetheless, a forensic analysis of the bones offered a unique zoo-archaeological opportunity to learn about horses in eighteenth-century Virginia. Centuries-old horse skeletons are rarely found; archaeologically this find had the potential to shed some light on Colonial equestrian history. Our analysis could determine the species, sex, age, stature, and general health of the Jamestown equine as well as some information of its life history. It was a male who died at age ..., ... hands high ... and it that had been afflicted with .... It also was either a riding horse or a coach horse because there was no sign of the type of joint stress that a work horse would develop. DNA analysis could determine its geographic origin but that test waits for future analysis. And the question of why this horse wound up buried in the churchyard boundary ditch remains unanswered.[23]

While the horse discovery failed to shed new light on the James Fort story, the archaeology of the "reduced" Fort certainly does. Now the archaeological remains of a rather intricate designed James Fort provide a more complete kaleidoscopic backdrop upon which the English men and women, Virginia Indians, and the famous Pocahontas, played out the events that wound up being significant first elements of the American experience. Yet there is more of the James Fort story to be told. Ten percent of the interior of the triangular Fort and the estimated one-acre area of the "reduced" Fort to the east are yet remains to be seen. So are the lost remains of one of the people who visited, lived in, and was married in the Fort: the Indian "Princess," Pocahontas.

Notes

1 Samuel Yonge, *Site of Old James Towne, Association for the Preservation of Virginia Antiquities* (Richmond, 1904), 34.
2 John L. Cotter, *Archeological Excavations at Jamestown Virginia* (Washington, DC: National Park Service, 1958), 166.
3 Philip Barbour, *The Complete Works of Captain John Smith* (Chapel Hill: University of North Carolina Press, 1986), I. 234.
4 See Chapter VII.
5 Barbour. Smith, II, 169.

6 Thanks to Barry Tsireston.

7 E. Tension, *Elizabethan England: Being the History of this Country "In Relation to all Foreign Princes"* (Dove with Griffin, Warwick, Great Britain, 1937).

8 Warner F. Gookin, *Bartholomew Gosnold* (London: Archon Books, 1963), 140.

9 Sarah M. Kingsbury, *The Records of the Virginia Company* (Washington, DC: United States Printing Office, 1933), I. 317.
   For discussions of Irish precedents for Virginia fortifications, see J. Reps, *Tidewater Towns* (Williamsburg, VA: The Colonial Williamsburg Foundation, 1972), passim; and I Noel Hume, *Martin's Hundred* (New York, 1991), C. Hodges, *Private Fortifications* report (1993), and Nicholas Luccketti, *Jamestown Rediscovery IV* (Richmond, VA, 2004), 43–44.

10 Paul Ives, *The Practice of Fortification* (London, 1589), 8.

11 Ibid.

12 See William Kelso, *Jamestown The Buried Truth* (2006) and *Jamestown, The Truth Revealed* (Charlottesville, VA, 2017), passim.

13 Ives, Practice, 8.

14 Ralph Hamor, *A True Discourse of the Present Estate of Virginia* (Richmond, 1957).

15 Kelso, op. cit.

16 Hamor, op. cit., Danny Schmidt personal communication.

17 Hamor. op.cit., Danny Schmidt personal communication.

18 William Kelso and Beverley Straube, *Jamestown Rediscovery VIII* (Association of the Preservation of Virginia Antiquities, 2004), 186.

19 Gravenhage Colectie Luepe Supplement Algemeernrijksarchief, The Hague, Velh 619.89.

20 Wright, op. cit., 63–64.

21 Barbour, Smith, II, 138, 140.

22 Ibid. Vol II, p. 225.

23 Jenna Kay Carlson, *Preliminary Report: Analysis of the Horse Skeleton Recovered from Jamestown Island, Virginia* (College of William and Mary Department of Anthropology, 2014).

3

POCAHONTAS, "A VIRGINIA LADY BORNE"

Since 1994, we Jamestown Rediscovery archaeologists have uncovered artifact-rich cellars, pits, and wells at the Fort. These held hundreds of thousands of early seventeenth-century English as well as an unparalleled early seventeenth-century Indian object collection. Of course, many of these Indian artifacts were acquired by the colonists in trade but the unprecedented magnitude of the collection suggests there was much more interaction and familiarity between the two groups within the Fort than historians had previously imagined.[1]

Virginia Indian *men* were well-documented visitors to James Fort, with some reported to have lived among the colonists. And aside from Pocahontas, Virginia Indian women were scarcely mentioned in association with the English settlement. However, one letter from the Spanish ambassador to England, Pedro de Zuniga, sent to the Spanish King, Charles II, indicated that "40 to 50 of the settlers had married with the Indians" by 1610. Zuniga was likely exaggerating the numbers as part of his campaign to infuriate the King enough to order the destruction of Jamestown before it could be permanently seated. Zuniga also more than once warned Charles that if the settlement of Jamestown took root, it would become a port from which English privateers could prey on Spanish gold-laden galleons as they sailed by the mouth of the James River from Central America. Yet neither the ploy about the intermarriages at Jamestown nor any other reasons goaded Charles into destroying the colony.

But the strong archaeological evidence of Indian women in the Fort is clear. For instance, a staggering amount of native ceramics, objects traditionally made by Indian women, were found throughout the Fort site, strong evidence of the Indian presence. Also women made shell beads which must account for the archaeological recovery of over 2,000 mussel shell bead blanks and the stone drills used to make them. An Indian pottery bowl was found sealed in a Fort building cellar hearth still

DOI: 10.4324/9781003441670-3

resting on the cooking fire ashes. The butchered bones of a large turtle and a pig lay nearby. So this was probably a space used as a kitchen. Since Indian women did the cooking in Indian society, it seems to be especially strong evidence that they were indeed living and working in the Fort.

From records, we can know the name of one of the women who came to the Fort, Pocahontas. She often brought the food that saved the starving settlers at crucial times. In 1613, she was held in the Fort for ransom in an attempt by Gov. Dale to trade her to Powhatan in exchange for stolen weapons. Powhatan never produced the ransom but during Pocahontas's captivity she was baptized and married to English planter, John Rolfe, in the church at Jamestown on April 1614. Virginia's investors saw great value in the conversion and marriage of Pocahontas. To the English, she was an Indian "princess" who was living proof that the native people of Virginia could be converted to Christianity and English ways. To the Indians, by her marriage to an Englishman, Jamestown became another matrilineal-led town in Powhatan's chiefdom.

In 1616, Pocahontas under her new married name, Rebecca Rolfe, went to England with her husband and young child, Thomas, to promote the Virginia colony and the companies' success at melding the English and Indian cultures. Under the care of the Virginia Governor for life, Sir Thomas West, and Lord De La Warre, she was an instant celebrity in London where the aristocracy and gentry flocked to see her.[2] She was introduced to King James, and as a celebrity when she attended a Royal spectacular masque. But her stardom did not last long. After Rolfe, Rebecca (Pocahontas), and their son Thomas spent also a year in England, the Company was hard put to keep up the families' expensive life style. They could no longer pay to show her off as a symbol of the Virginia Company success in such an expensive city. Soon "though sore against her will," Pocahontas and her son boarded the ship *George* in March 1617 bound for Virginia.[3] She never made it out of the Thames, dying of an unknown illness on the ship as it sailed down the river on its way to Virginia. She was taken to the nearest town, Gravesend, and buried on March 21, aged 22 years. However, her death and her burial did not end her story.

Today, the *exact* burial location of Pocahontas is lost to history. We do know this: according to the St. Georges Church Register, on March 21, 1616/17 "Rebecca Rolfe [her Christian married name] wife of Thomas Rolfe [John Rolfe] a Virginia lady borne [was] buried in the chancel."[4] This and all other burial entries in the register are in past tense so they are very likely trustworthy records of the actual interment events. So Pocahontas's body almost certainly was placed in the timber St. Georges Church chancel. But since her burial, the St. Georges register ends with this terse entry: "Fire at Gravesend Augt. 1727 at which time the old church and the greatest part of the Town was consumed." The extent of the fire damage was severe including monuments and gravestones that were defaced and consumed.

After the fire, the original church was considered irreparable so the parishioners circulated a partition to raise money for a completely new structure.[5] Fortunately about the time of the St Georges fire, Queen Anne funded a campaign to build a

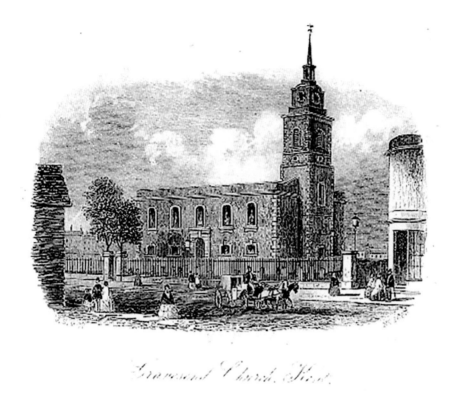

FIGURE 3.1 The 1732 redesigned and rebuilt St. Georges Church, Gravesend.

Source: Douglas Grier, Gravesend Borough Council.

number of elaborate churches in London and in the vicinity of London. As a part of that initiative, the Crown funded a new and much upgraded St. Georges Church which was built soon after 1732.[6]

As a result of these two ground-disturbing events, the fire and new construction, the location of the original chancel and consequently Pocahontas's exact buried place became lost.

This loss, it seemed to me, when I first heard about it from the St Georges vicar in 1994, was tragic since Pocahontas had played such a major role in Jamestown story.[7] I thought it is fitting that someone should find her grave so it could be properly marked and memorialized. I decided I would give it a try. That goal led me on a 20-year circuitous journey to consider all relevant evidence of the whereabouts or even the destruction of her remains, no matter how seemingly credible or fanciful they may be. This included finds in the British National and County Record Offices, the basement of London Museum of Natural History, various British and American newspaper records, eighteenth-century books, the Gravesend Library, interviews with the St. Georges Church clergy, and a ground-penetrating radar study of the St. Georges Church interior in collaboration with the Museum of London Archaeological Service. The results of those efforts follow.

A Gravesend historian/scientist, Robert Pocock re-published a detailed visitation report by John Thorpe[8] that listed all the burial memorials and ledger stones in the chancel and nave in St. George's chapel that existed before the 1727 fire.[9] He names approximately 18 people who were memorialized in the chancel in the period 1609–1675. One can assume that the memorials of these deceased people and/or their family members were likely buried in pre-constructed family vaults. Further, it is apparent from the way Thorpe and Pocock grouped the names there were a total of three family vaults, one for six Robertson family members, one for two of the Ward family, and twelve for the Bere family. Thorpe does not mention any marker for Rebecca Rolfe (Pocahontas).

Since the register establishes that Pocahontas was "buried" in the chancel, the lack of a memorial strongly suggests that she was not laid away in a vault. This is not surprising since the church elders unexpectedly faced the task of burying a "Lady" with very short notice and with no time and presumably no Virginia Company funds to build a new vault. Further, it is particularly significant that Pocock adds to the historical narrative when he wrote that the practice of intramural church burials ended with the construction of the existing Queen Anne church.[10] So any graves or family burial vaults that existed in the previous buried church would be built over after 1732 and would date before 1727, the date of the fire. If Rebecca Rolfe/Pocahontas was likely not buried in a vault because of lack of time and money but rather buried directly in chancel ground, or even if she was buried in a non-commemorated vault, the original place of her interment would be sealed beneath the new church by 1732.

While it seems unlikely that Pocahontas was buried in a vault, there is some reason to think she was. A reference written by John H. Haslam rector of St. Georges 1892–1899 states:

> the clergyman of St Georges was Nicholas Frankwell" "... who is believed to be the person who permitted Pocahontas to be buried in the rectors vault. [Further] there were two vaults under the floor. One is the rector's vault and the other is the Robinson vault for that family.[11]

Haslam also stated that the burial of St. Georges Rector, John Hughes, and his wife was in the Rector's vault presumably with Pocahontas.[12] However, there is no reference in the church register to a "Rector's vault" nor a vault that also held Pocahontas' remains.[13]

Another secondary reference to the St. Georges chancel burials reads: "*In 1892 during the chancel expansion, two coffins were discovered but found to be empty. That same year, two coffins came to light under the East Window, but whatever their contents, no record was made.*" The author, Francis Mossiker, states that according to some unnamed reference: "*The stained glass east window, comes from the old chancel and was presented by Col. Gladdish in 1866 in memory of his wife Elizabeth.*"[14] Both references together seem to imply that Mossiker thought the contents of the "emptied chancel coffins" were moved to be reburied in the late nineteenth century beneath the "old chancel" window, presumably salvaged from the 1727 fire. Also she seems to imply because the recycled "old" window from the original church marked it then perhaps the remains of Pocahontas wound up there as well. However, it seems almost certain judging from the church ledger entry describing the magnitude of the church fire and the statement by Pocock that the fire was hot enough to even destroy stone commemorative "vault markers" that any stained glass windows would be completely melted away. That is, if there were any.

There is, however, stronger but still speculative evidence that, in time, Rebecca's remains were recovered from a chancel vault, and then reburied in a vault outside the new 1732 church. But that, it can be concluded, was not a final resting place. According to one account, the remains were recovered again when the church was enlarged in 1897 during which time bones were moved yet again, to be re-reburied in the southwest corner of the St. George's graveyard.[15]

About or soon after 1897, Rev. Haslam wrote on the inside cover of the St Georges Church Register about the alleged effects of the fire on chancel burials and the whereabouts of the remains of Pocahontas.[16] Even though the register cover had become deteriorated and discarded when the register went to the Medway Record Office for safe-keeping, the Home Office secretary, Henry Gladstone, quoted it on Jan 30, 1923:

> … when clearing away the debris after the fire of 1727 partly burned bones found in the chancel apparently were deposited in a vault in the churchyard on the north side of the church, for in 1892 when the Apse was enlarged and rebuilt, careful search was made, traces of vaults were found but there was nothing in them. When the North Aisle was built in 1897 the graves in the ground taken in were emptied and in one vault a quantity of partly burned bones was found, evidently the bones removed from the vaults of the original chancel after the fire. These were again deposited in a vault in the S.W. corner of the churchyard twenty and one half feet from the S. wall and twenty-five feet from the W. wall as per plan [sketch plan was enclosed].

"The name on the plan [vault] is that of Curd." Reverend Gedge also added that the last Curd interment was made in 1804 and that

> … it was common knowledge that the grave was not really a vault but a brick grave with a loose slab was previously to its being used for a "the receptacle of rubbish swept from the surrounding ground. As I learned from the aged women who was then caretaker that some controversy arose at the time of the insertion of this note in the register [Haslam's note] whether the grave indicated or one

in its neighborhood was the one used for the calculated bones, ... [in a letter written two months later Gedge added] "... request the leave given us may be inclusive enough to permit our making some search if the Curd grave proves empty ... to take up the uninscribed stone to the immediate eastward of the Curd grave twenty feet from the south wall and twenty five feet from the west wall of the churchyard ... .[17]

It appears that Gedge was far more dubious as to the location of the reburial vault of the burned bones, than Haslam. But the Home Office only issued a license for opening the Curd vault.

In any case, Haslam concluded that the empty burial vaults found in 1727 once held the burned bones of people buried in the "original" chancel. His conclusion appears to be based on the fact that the vaults were empty in 1892 and that the buried bones (he?) found in 1897 that were reburied in a "vault" north of the present church had come from that primary burial in the empty chancel vaults *because* they were burned during the fire of 1727. In other words, Haslam concluded the reburied burned bones outside the church must have come from the original church chancel vault that was found to be empty and the proof lay in the fact that they were burned. However, there is no contemporary record of any removal of chancel vault burials after the 1727 fire before they were likely built over by the construction of the 1732 replacement church.

Given there is a leap of faith from fire to final reburial, in all fairness, Haslam's thrice removal and reburial scenario *seems* plausible. The St. George's parishioners or relatives of people buried in the chancel vaults might have reverently recovered and removed the original burials from these vault structures. They were likely intact in the ground beneath the church ashes before construction digging on the site for foundation of the new church could disturb or even desecrate them. But how could they been burned? It is difficult to explain how bones lying below the church floor in what had to be masonry vaults could wind up being charred from the heat of a fire that had burned above them. Heat rises.

Still, Haslam must be right about one thing, the vaults he found beneath the Apse construction dated to the time when the original church chancel existed. Remember Pocock reported that according to church rules, no burials could be made inside the new 1732 church. So are Haslam's conclusions without a doubt? No. Again just because we can know from what must be a reliable source, the church register, that Pocahontas was buried in the chancel 1616/17, it would be a giant leap of faith that the burned bones Haslam found buried outside the church had actually come from the empty original chancel vaults. Actually, these remains could be from other people burned by the fire in the town (above ground) and then buried in a chancel vault.[18]

There is other evidence that Russell's story may not be credible. Despite the indisputable church register entry that "Rebecca" was a chancel burial, there is some evidence that Pocahontas was subsequently reburied not in the southwest corner of the graveyard but rather in the northwest corner. According to a 1881 letter written by P.G. Robert, an American visitor to Gravesend church, published in the Richmond Dispatch newspaper:

Reported successively from age to age.

[I have learned] … in Gravesend that Pocahontas was buried in the northwest corner of the church-yard, at a spot to which the sexton led us. It was just next a tombstone on which we deciphered 'Wife of John Weed. July –, 1329,' or 1529, possibly. This certainly establishes the antiquity of burials in that part of the yard, whether the date above be of the fourteenth or the sixteenth century. This sexton (Tomas Turner) has been in office nine years. He received the tradition of the spot from his predecessor, William Netteingham, who was sexton for about twenty years. William received it from his father, John Netteingham, who was clerk of the parish for fifty-two years. This carries back the account more than eighty years, for John Netteingham told his son, William, that all his life from his boyhood that spot had been pointed out as the one near which 'or about at which' Pocahontas was buried. In the absence, then, of all proof 'upon record,' this tradition comes to us nearly an established fact as possible, without an exhumation and a recover of the remains or of some relics identifying them.[19]

One could conclude from this letter the identification of Pocahontas' burial place in the northwest corner of the churchyard goes back to at least 1793, or earlier, when the elder Netteingham was the church sexton (9 years plus 22 years, plus 52 years equals 88 years). It is also likely that if the elder Netteingham had heard the story from his father when he was a boy, which is extremely likely, the account could go back another 20 years, to 1773 when eye-witnesses of the church fire could still be alive to tell firsthand, about its effect, if any, on the church chancel burials. They also could have witnessed any removal of bones from the original chancel to a reburial place in the northwest corner of the graveyard.

But it could be that the 1881 Gravesend visitor, Mr. Roberts, did not know north from south when he was in the graveyard and that he was being shown the *southwest* and not the *northwest* corner. That would confirm Russell's southwestern location for the final reburial of the burned bones in Curd's tomb. But that does not work chronologically. Haslam wrote that he moved the burned bones to Curd's tomb in 1897, 16 years after Tomas Tuner showed Roberts the northwestern location of Pocahontas' grave. So this earlier story by Turner could in fact corroborate Haslam's story about the original chancel vaults being empty and the bones removed from the chancel after the fire and reburied but it does not validate that Curd's tomb was the final resting place for the "positively" identified burned bones.

Gedge's letter with the transcribed Haslam story was part of an effort to get permission from the British Home Office to search for and recover Pocahontas's remains in the St. George's churchyard. That effort was spearheaded by a Captain E.P.

Gaston, an art historian and museum curator who was the president of an organization known as the English-Speaking Union. He eventually recruited a prestigious team of experts: Mr. W.P. Pycraft, Assistant Keeper of the Zoological Department of the British Museum, Sir Arthur Keith of the Royal College of Surgeons, as well as Gedge and Kent archaeologist, Coyler-Ferguson. The group did focus their search on the Curd's tomb, the vault that Haslam specifically pinpointed by his map.

But that is getting ahead of the story. Some 14 years before the English-Speaking Union's search to find Pocahontas' presumed thrice buried burned bones, a prestigious group known as the Pocahontas Memorial Association had applied to the Home Office for permission to exhume Pocahontas and return her to America. The Association letterhead lists 100 prominent American men that made up the Association's Board of Directors including none other than Theodore Roosevelt, Henry Cabot Lodge, Grover Cleveland, Alexander Graham Bell, and numerous mayors, bank presidents, members of the U.S. Congress, bishops, presidents of various Colleges and Heritage groups. The first letter written (1909) from the Association secretary from a Mr. E. St. John Matthews to Gladstone proposed the following:

> It is the intention of the ... Association to erect a magnificent memorial to Princess Pocahontas in our National Capital, Washington, D.D [sic]. In the center of that memorial will be a large crypt for the remains of the princess if a thorough and systematic search [for the remains] is successful. We would like to know from you [how to obtain] ... permission ... to bring them [the remains] to this country ... and if you can advise us in any way the best method to take to find the remains we would be very grateful. If we are successful ... [we would jointly] have a warship of each country escort the remains ... an international event that we think would do more to bind the friendship existing between the two countries than any other event of the past century. For after all our country is Anglo-Saxon in the language and its ideals and bringing back to the country of her birth of the remains of Pocahontas would make our people realize [that]as nothing else would or could.[20]

Gladstone referred the letter to an assistant, "JP," who recorded his reaction and advice in the Home Office minutes. First, he sarcastically wrote: *"This is an amusing application. The writer does not appear himself to have taken any trouble to discover the facts as to the death of Pocahontas and the disposal of her remains."* The rest of the report appears to be more tongue-in-cheek reaction including the conclusion that *"... the writer [of the Application] is rather an irresponsible person judging by the magnificent non-sequitur of his final paragraph." "For after all our country is Anglo-Saxon ... etc."* However, JP did admit *"the Association is an impressive one"*[21] so there was some attempt to find out what was known about Pocahontas's exact burial place by the H. O. The Office did learn she was indeed buried in a church at Gravesend that was razed and then built over and also that the Borough Librarian there, Mr. A. Philip *"... has investigated the question and collected all that is known as to the death and interment of the Princess."* He also discovered that Philips had written "all that he knew" in his forthcoming article in The Home Counties Magazine of November 1909.[22] Philips subsequently offered to send a synopsis of his article to the Association.

What prompted Philips' article was in reaction to a news story about "*the discovery of human remains, pronounced by an expert to be those of an Indian female of high degree, [found] near the site of the old Chapel of St. Mary, Graves-end who some had concluded must be the remains of Pocahontas ... ."* He continued that the discovery "*... has nothing to settle the old dispute as to the burial of Pocahontas ... "*[23] He identified the Chapel of St. Mary as the official Chapel of the small village of Gravesend until that function transferred to St. Georges Church about a mile to the northeast in 1544. He went on to speculate that it was in the Graveyard of St. Mary's that Pocahontas was interred in spite of the register entry that she was buried in the St. George's Chancel. His conclusion was based on the fact that the St. Mary's Chapel was still standing in 1617 and he accepted the tradition that Pocahontas died of some highly contagious disease, probably smallpox. So because of contagion he decided she had to be buried in an isolated place like St. Mary's graveyard and not in the very public St. George's

FIGURE 3.2   W.P. Pycraft measures Curd's tomb skulls that were removed from Curd's tomb.

Chancel in town. Yet his opening statement contradicts that conclusion. He wrote that the "Indian remains" found presumably at the St. Mary's graveyard site did nothing to "settle" the dispute about the burial place of Pocahontas. If he thought she was buried there, then why not assume that Indian remains found in that graveyard might be hers? In any event, it appears that what he wrote put to rest the Association's interest in finding and returning Pocahontas to the U.S.

Philips' theory published in 1909 about Pocahontas's St. Mary's burial had no effect on the proposed 1923 Curd's tomb excavation where, as we have seen, there was convincing evidence pinpointing Pocahontas's final resting place in the St. Georges graveyard. The Curd vault was opened on May 30, under the pressure of sensational and unwanted press coverage. The report reads: *"... in an hour or so they were completely surprised when it proved to be full of skeletons and all manner of other things."* "They reportedly then cleared away the rubbish and the human remains then rapidly reburied."[24] But another account states that Mr. Pycraft and probably Sir Arthur Keith were given an extra day to look for indications among the bones they had recovered for the presence of Indian characteristics on the skulls (high cheekbones) and a "ring" for which they somehow had a reference. Then five skulls were found to be "of sufficient interest" to take away which were ultimately deposited in the London Museum of Natural History.

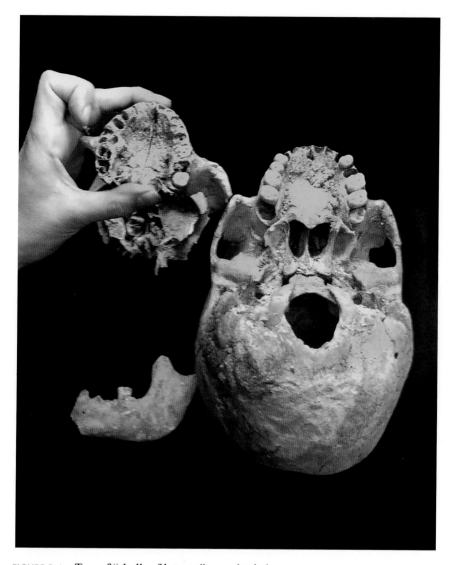

FIGURE 3.4 Two of "skulls of interest" not reburied.

Source: Deposited in the London Museum of Natural History collections (JRF).

A brief handwritten report by Pycraft filed at the LMNH reads:

"W.P. Pycraft Report,
London Museum of Natural History:
Gravesend
Skulls From St. Georges Church
Gravesend"

30.V.23 These Skulls were taken from a brick-grave in the course of a search for the body of "Princess Pocahontas" It was thought that her body was exhumed from the chancel of the old Church & thrown into this grave with some 200 other bodies. After the search had ended, unsuccessfully, an "old inhabitant" came forward with the Statement that as a boy he remembered the Enlargement of the existing (?) Church, & told Pycraft that at that time (?) "Series of Bodies" were dug up, which had been buried just inside its walls. There, after lying exposed for some time [they] were at last thrown into the brick grave where they were found. The body of "Pocahontas" it was known was buried in the Chancel of the original church, destroyed by fire. It probably remains there, but the site of the chancel is unknown. The five skulls brought away were of sufficient interest to warrant there being brought away.[25]

The exhumation was carried out under the supervision of the writer (W. P. Pycraft) and Sir Arthur Kent of the College of Surgeons.

At that time as it would be today, investigating such a high-profile burial created a press feeding frenzy, just what the research group wanted to avoid. In reading through the exchange of letters between the Home Office and the researchers, it is clear that the beginning was fairly tranquil but a learning curve developed as the Home Office began to realize how strong negative public reaction could be. It ranged from irate members of Pocahontas's husband family, the Rolfes, to people that believed disturbing any grave was sacrilege or pointless. Over the space of the first six months, the project went from an inspired idea of Gaston and Reverend Gedge (who was in fact physically blind and apparently blind to potential public opinion) to a barrage of outrage fueled by wildly inaccurate but sensational press stories. A few examples:

Headlines: **Exhuming a Red Indian Princess**, Evening News, 30.5.23; **100 Skeletons Dug UP, Search for the Bones of a Princess**, Daily Express, 31.5.1923; **Vault Search, Exhumation of USA Princess**, Daily News, 31.5.23; **Tomb's Secret, Surprising Discovery of Bones of 50 People**, Daily Chronicle, 31.5.23; **Dead Mrs. Rolfe**, *"They laid her in a tomb under the chancel ... such a tomb as a gentlemen's wife should have ... and there if her coffin escaped the fire, she must be lying until this day ... this [excavation] is a meddling curiosity, a peeping curiosity,"* Evening News, 31.5.23; **Pocahontas Ghouls, Antiquarianism Run Riot**, *"a lot of ghouls ... searching among debris for a skull with black hair on it,"* Daily Express, 6.1.23; **Princesses Tomb Secret, Skulls of Red Indian Type Found At Gravesend**, The Londoner, 5.31.23: *Princesses Tomb Search Complete Story by the Men Responsible, For America?,* *"Might be Indian skulls ... one or two skulls that might conceivably belonged to American Indians,... these also were reinterred."* Evening News 6.1.23; **Echo of the 17th Century**, Daily Mirror 6.1.23; **Digging for Dead Princess, Hunt for Princesses Body**, *"Church Wardens dissociate themselves from any responsibly [for the excavation] ... They express disgust that any grave should be disturbed,"* Daily news, 6.1.23; **Poor Pocahontas**, *"it is easy to understand the kind of reverence which desecrates what it seeks to honour, and finds its highest act of worship in a business which would sicken a scavenger,* ... Pocahontas, An Increasing Mystery "[on the bones] ... no signs of ... of incineration was encountered." "Thus instead of solving the Pocahontas legend, the outcome of our efforts at identification has simply increased the original mystery,"* Illustrated London News 6.2.23.[26]

Another news story which was probably quite farfetched appeared in the London Daily Express three days after the excavation with this headline: **Princess for a Balloon, Were Pocahontas' Bones Barter by Children?**

[The bones of] Princess Pocahontas, the pretty Red Indian may have been sold to a rag and bone man for a balloon. The bones in the Gravesend church yard disinterred by ... Gaston, the distinguished American archaeologist, were originally dug up fifty years ago [during church construction] ... and thrown aside. Children from the village ... took away all the bones they could carry and sold them [for] balloons. There was a great hue and cry. The ... rag and bone man's ... cart was searched [the bones] were returned and were buried in a hastily dug pit in the churchyard. It is this pit recently searched for remains. Daily Express, 6.2.23.

A week after the vault excavation, a rather astonishing letter postmarked New York, N.Y. from Mrs. J W Fowler, (50 church street), suite 383, to the Home Office testifies to another very questionable resting place for Pocahontas:

hearing some American tourists in London were searching in the cemetary (sic) of Gravesend at St Georges chapel for the remains of Pocahontas can tell you on pretty good authority the remains were brought to America by some English people and buried on the out skirts of N Y city. If they would care to know further particulars [I]would be most pleased to hear from you.[27]

It is interesting and perhaps significant that the address, 50 church street, at that time apparently was an apartment complex adjacent to St, Paul's Cathedral and graveyard. While this is hardly on the "outskirts of town," Mrs. Fowler may have heard a "rumor" about Pocahontas's burial in New York but she named the wrong cemetery since she probably thought St. Paul's would make much more sense for the burial of a "princess." The purported oldest cemetery in New York, Prospect Cemetery, is located in East Queens which could be considered to be on the outskirts of the city at that time. At any rate, the people at the Home Office did not consider this letter to have validity. Probably by that point, they must have had quite enough of the burial place of Pocahontas as they did not ask Ms. Fowler for "particulars." Attached to the letter is a note simply directing RSK? To *"lay by" 18/6/23.*

By 1932, tales of the whereabouts of Pocahontas' remains continued to go way beyond the bounds of Gravesend. A story in the London Times of November 18 reads: *"permission has been granted to the rector of Heacham, Norfolk ... to erect a monument in the church to the Indian Princess Pocahontas ... who was buried there."* The article goes on to refute itself by adding that while the Heacham Church was the pre-Jamestown church of the John Rolfe, Pocahontas' husband, *"... she [Pocahontas] was buried at Gravesend."* While this story explains the error, its appearance in the press prompted another unfounded tale locating Pocahontas's remains in London.

On November 24, the Times received a letter claiming that in 1872 the unnamed writer's great uncle, the verger [caretaker] of St, John, *"... took him to the vaults in the crypt and showed him resting on a shelf, a silver casket, somewhat dirty."* A plate stated that it had been interred at Gravesend and brought up on a barge and had been exhibited at a show, but the authorities had placed it [back] in the crypt and that the casket contained the body of an American Indian princess. Inspection of the crypt by the writer was abortive but yet another newspaper article reads: *"18 January 1835 the favorite squaw of an Indian chief who came to London died at her lodgings in the Waterloo road. ... she was buried in an elegant black coffin ... at St John's Waterloo road."* While the St. John's Church register has no entry for Pocahontas, there was another story stating *"... 18 January, 1835, the favored squaw of an Indian chief, died this day. Her name was ah-mik-waw-begum-o-."* So it seems by 1872 the coffin of the squaw had become the coffin of Pocahontas in the mind of the great uncle of the unknown author and the "silver coffin" had tarnished to "elegant black."

More abortive searches. Wayne Newton, a famous wealthy American vocalist and Virginia Indian ancestor of Pocahontas, felt that Pocahontas' expatriation burial at Gravesend was an atrocity. So he made another attempt to find her remains in 1997–2000. Just like the 1909 Pocahontas Association, he wanted to find her so that he could bring her back "home." But this time "home" would not be a spectacular mausoleum in Washington, D.C. but rather the Virginia Pamunkey Indian Reservation. This proper reburial at her former home, according to Newton and Virginia Indian tradition, would assure that her soul could finally rest. Newton, like Gaston, recruited a "dream team" of experts to analyze her remains, Dr. Henry Lee, noted forensic anthologist, New York pathologist Michael Baden, and British coroner, Peter Dean. However, they soon ran into the same old problem; her exact burial place inside the St. Georges Church or graveyard was unknown. *"We aren't sure where her bones are. We believe she may be underneath the church, but without digging up the whole thing they'll never find ... [the bones]"* According to church authorities, that complete "fishing" excavation could never happen. Apparently, Newton and his team gave up their quest when they saw that a total excavation of the entire interior of the St. Georges Church or any graveyard digging would be more than a daunting task and it became clear that the local and Church of England authorities would almost certainly not allow it.

Not knowing anything about the various stories of searches and theories about Pocahontas' exact burial place at Gravesend, I first visited the St. Georges Church in the 1990s in order to see what must be some visual marker of her exact burial place in the church. Rector Willey could not point that place out but he assured me that she was buried somewhere in the church chancel. As an archaeologist, such an answer did not satisfy me and I thought that maybe I could find out at least a documentary record of her burial place. So in 2000, I sent an inquiry to the British Museum seeking any records of the 1923 Gaston search in the churchyard and the whereabouts of the five skulls "… of sufficient interest" wound up. They passed me on to the London Museum of Natural History. The first response to my enquiry from the NHML staff there was negative. They wrote that they had nothing relating to this excavation on file. A few days later, however, the staff did find some records in their archives that indicated that they did indeed have a number of skulls from the St. Georges excavation appropriately stored in a vault at the bottom of their WWII bomb-proof basement. After a visit proved that the remains were there, I arranged for a group of scholars sponsored by crime novelist, Patricia Cornwell, to bring Dr. Ashley McKeown, forensic anthropologist, to London to analyze the skulls. She comprehensively studied them and concluded that the individuals were all males and definitely not American Indians. But the existence of the skulls in the museum proved that Mr. Pycraft and his associates did indeed not rebury all the human remains removed from Curd's tomb in 1923, as he reported at first.

Given this documentary and archaeological record of the whereabouts of the grave of Pocahontas, there remain many unanswered questions.

1 Does the 1881 oral history story about Pocahontas's burial in the northwest corner of the churchyard refer to the original 1616/17 burial place? This must be a reference to a reburial because the seventeenth-century registry entry so precisely locates the original grave in the original chancel. So was this the actual location where the burned bones were "reburied" right after the 1727 fire?
2 In 1892, did Haslam actually see totally empty vaults under the present church?
3 How could the fire of 1727 burn downward into a closed vault and burn any bones at all? Were these really the remains of town people killed in the fire in 1727?
4 With only a few days' notice after her death, how could the church put Pocahontas in a chancel vault? Vaults were usually built at great expense by and for local families. With so little advance notice, wouldn't she be buried in the chancel in "un-occupied" ground instead of in a vault?
5 Were the vault remains actually reburied in the churchyard? Further, were the reburials of partially burned bones, which may have been removed because of the 1897 expansion of the church apse, actually from the first 1727 churchyard reburial?
6 Are the late nineteenth-century accounts based on reasonably credible 300-year-old oral history or just myth?
7 What led Rev. Haslam to think that the alleged pre-1727 chancel reburials that were moved again in 1897 wound up in Curd's tomb?

8 Why were there so many skeletons redeposited in Curd's tomb along with domestic trash?

9 What were the criteria used by Keith and/or Pycraft to save the Natural History Museum skulls? Why did others involved with the project state that all the remains were reburied when clearly the skulls were taken away?

After reviewing all the stories about the location today of Pocahontas's remains, I decided to arrange for a ground penetrating radar study (GPR) inside the current church which might, I thought, define the plan of the pre-1727 church and at least locate its buried chancel. That study was conducted under the aegis of The Museum of London in 2010. The outcome was disappointing. The archaeologists concluded that it was apparent the GPR search did not detect any remains of the pre-fire church or its chancel. They further concluded that the radar waves seemed to be blocked by a scrambled layer of rubble possibly from the leveling of the original church foundation that had been spread out during the 1731 construction of the present stone church. On the other hand, the GPR did show what appears to be a division line just south of the present chancel and apse which just may be a foundation line dividing the original chancel from the nave. If that is true and if Pocahontas was buried in the chancel ground and likely not in a vault, then her remains still lie undisturbed and for sure unburned, in the ground probably on the left (west) side of what is now near the chancel. Excavation in the future remains to be seen.

Notes

1 Mark Summers, Jamie May, *The World of Pocahontas* (Jamestown Archaearium Museum exhibit).
2 Tim Hashaw, Investigative Reporter email exchange.
3 John Chamberlain letter to Dudley Carleton, Ruth Selmon, *Pocahontas in London* (The National Archives, catalogue reference: SP 14/90, f.56).
4 St. Georges Register of Burials, Medway Council Archives (Richmond, UK). Journalist Tim Hashaw thinks that because John Rolfe was not with Pocahontas when she died and was buried, therefore the register got his name confused with their son Peter.
5 Robert Pocock, *The History of Gravesend and Milford* (Gravesend, 1797), 74.
6 M. H. Port, ed., *The Commissions for Building Fifty New Churches. The Minute Books, 1711–27: A Calendar* (London Record Society, 23, 1986).
7 St. Georges' rector, David Willey, stated to me, "She is in glory with God no matter where her bones are buried."
8 Thorpe, John. Registrum Roffense, or, "A collection of antient records, charters, and instruments of divers kinds: necessary for illustrating the ecclesiastical history and antiquities of the diocese and cathedral church of Rochester" 1682–1750, pp. 748–750: Tim Hashaw alerted me to this reference.
9 Ibid., Pocock and Thorp. Passim.
10 Ibid., Pocock, 74.
11 Charles Ap Thomas, *Ye True Narrative of ye Princess Pocahontas* (Matoaka, 1897), 26.
12 Hashaw email 7.29.17.
13 Op. cit. St. Georges Church Register.

14 Francis Mossiker, Pocahontas, Her Life and Legend (1976), 284.
15 Rev. Haslam, Rector of St. Georges from 1892 to 1898 wrote the note according to Tim Hashaw who generously shared his research.
16 Russel was not the author according to Hashaw.
17 The National Archives, Kew, UK, Home Office (HO), 176060, HO 45/14558 5935 47.
18 Hashaw.
19 P.G. Robert, Richmond Dispatch newspaper (Volume 60, Number 62, 10 September), Report, London Natural History Museum, basement vault.
20 Op. cit, Home Office.
21 Ibid.
22 Home County Magazine. np.
23 Ibid.
24 W.P. Pycraft Report, London Natural History Museum, basement vault.
25 Ibid.
26 All of these news stories were taken from copies of newspaper clippings collected, archived and shared by the Home Office.
27 Op. cit. Home Office.

4

FORT TO PORT

Historical archaeologists do indeed go through layers of buried things as they dig backward in time, from the present to all of the past. While the foremost goal of the Jamestown Rediscovery Archaeological Project was to uncover the earliest and generally the deepest remains of the "lost" seventeenth-century James Fort, we had to dig through more recent remains to get there. Simply throwing aside deposits that accumulated on the site since the Fort Period (1607–1624), however, would be an unacceptable archaeological practice. After all, history is a continuum. Consequently, we made every attempt to carefully record later deposits before or as they had to be removed. If they were not superimposed on the earlier deposits, they were left undisturbed and preserved for the future.

Our archaeological excavations did indeed discover levels and deposits of the "lost" Fort, but beyond that, we also discovered the foundations of two mid-seventeenth-century burned buildings: one straddling the abandoned southeast fort bulwark ditch, and the other a house ruin in the middle of the James Fort site (Figure 2.1). Other "newer" discoveries included the remains of two post-supported structures: one with a shallow cellar, plus two wells and signs of garden enclosures. Together these archaeological components reflected Jamestown's evolution from an initial military base and trading post to a residential, commercial river port that became known as "James Citty." Simply put, the change was literally from fort to port.

Jamestown, the port, was the on-again off-again hub of a lucrative Virginia tobacco trade. That "cash crop" formed the basis of the colony's economy. Tobacco "cash" was used to purchase both indentured servants and slaves to grow it. It was also used to pay taxes and tithes and to pay for imported English goods. Beginning in 1619, and then throughout the Colonial Period, Virginia General

DOI: 10.4324/9781003441670-4

FIGURE 4.1 Artist's conception of a scene at Jamestown, the seventeenth-century port.
Source: Courtesy the National Park Service.

Assembly legislation required official inspection of tobacco before it could be shipped to England. A number of official port towns and warehouses were appointed to implement tobacco laws. After 1631, however, legislation named Jamestown as the only Virginia port that could officially export tobacco in trade for English goods. This led to a boom in the town's development. Ironically, King James hated the "noxious weed," but he loved getting the tobacco taxes and the crop turned out to be the saving grace of the perpetually struggling Virginia colony. The focus on the Virginia tobacco cash crop had its drawbacks. In actual fact, it disrupted the overall growth and development of Virginia. Governor Berkeley put it this way: "This ... [tobacco] was the first and fundamental hindrance that made the planters neglect all other accessions to wealth and happiness, and fix their hopes only on this vicious weed of tobacco, they can neither handsomely subsist with it, nor without it."[1]

Despite Berkeley's criticism of the planters' tobacco obsession, the implementation of the government's tobacco legislation itself had an enormous impact on shaping the physical townscape of urban Jamestown. Merchants quickly patented land in town and soon began to build tobacco warehouses. One of these buildings left a major archaeological imprint on the riverbank near the seventeenth-century Jamestown church. As we uncovered the southeast James Fort bulwark moat, it soon became apparent that a substantial seventeenth-century building once stood there, after the bulwark had decayed away (Figures 4.2 and 4.3). The structure's siting at the water's edge and the configuration of the foundation that we uncovered left little doubt that these were the remnants of a dual-purpose warehouse/house. Records indicated that the building was almost certainly built by Jamestown merchant capitalist John White. His 1644 land patent gave two fairly precise locational references to his property: "... bounded west upon the Church Yard ... and south upon James river."[2]

These present-day known points of reference, the churchyard, and the river remain as precise "you-are-here" points, proving that the remains we found stood on property once owned by White.

We can know more about the man himself from other references, even though the name "John White" is almost as common an English name as John Smith. There are enough documentary references to a Jamestown resident John White from the 1640s and 1650s to strongly suggest he was the property owner near the church. And we can know something of his biography. He had been a politician as well as a multi-tasking Jamestown entrepreneur. In 1642, he served in the House

FIGURE 4.2 John White's ware/house site during excavation.

Source: David Doody, JRF.

FIGURE 4.3   Archaeological remains of John White's ware/house.

Source: Michael Lavin, JRF.

of Burgesses, and was also referred to as a "merchant of London and Virginia." In fact, he sold land that ultimately became the site of modern downtown Richmond in 1649. He also grew and shipped tobacco.[3]

The stone and brick foundation we found measured 30′ x 40′ overall, one of the largest structural foundations yet discovered at Jamestown.[4] The footing was made up of a single course of brick strengthened by a stone underpinning. This was a substantial foundation, but not robust enough to support a brick building. It could, however, support a heavy timber-framed structure that included two brick fireplaces along the west wall. We also uncovered brick building debris trailing away from the northern basement fireplace—brick likely randomly tossed there by salvagers sorting through a collapsed chimney pile while seeking re-useable bricks. Fortunately, removal of the scrambled brick revealed sections of the chimney stack lying where it had fallen, still bonded together. Despite the fact that the building had been leveled and much of the building materials carried off by the salvagers, this "horizontal" chimney provided much telling architectural evidence of the above-ground structure. The length of the mortared brick courses indicated that the former standing chimney had risen at least 26 feet high. That meant that the building had to have been one and one-half to two stories high, with at least two and perhaps three stacked fireplaces—one in the basement, and one each on the two levels above it. Such a sizeable building fits with the Jamestown building trend that Governor John Harvey described in 1638: "[There are} …twelve houses and stores built in the Towne, one of brick…the fairest that ever was known in this countrye … others have undertaken to build framed houses to beautifye the place, consonant to his majesties instruction that we should not suffer men to build slight cottages as heretofore."[5] In other words, White likely carried out this Governor's mandate.

Besides the fact that the size of White's structure appears exceptional for Jamestown, other signs indicate that the building was of high quality. We found a considerable number of pale yellow undersized "Dutch" bricks in the basement ruins. These specialty bricks were a prized commodity in the American colonial period. In New York and Delaware, colonists often used them for architectural decoration in highly visible places, particularly hearths and fireboxes. In fact, Dutch bricks were decorative enough to be specified in an elaborate Virginia graveyard monument. Richard Cole of Westmoreland County stipulated that he wanted his gravestone of black marble with a brass coat of arms to be "raised with Dutch bricks above three foot from the ground."[6] In addition to being used in White's house, these Dutch bricks were found on other key Jamestown buildings. They were used to pave a floor of the first statehouse built by Governor William Berkeley in the 1640s.[7] Other architectural artifacts besides the Dutch bricks indicate that White's warehouse was upscale. A considerable amount of ceramic roofing tiles were also found among the debris in the ruin. A tile roof was heavy, requiring a substantial timber-frame: far superior to the "slight cottages" common in Jamestown. We also found places in the warehouse/house basement free of brick rubble. In one place of particular significance, removal of debris exposed a section of charred wooden flooring (Figure 4.4).

The charred floorboards indicated that the building had been destroyed by fire. A burned timber was found socketed into the southern stonework foundation. This must have been a sill for an oversize door, ten feet wide, at the center of the south wall. This was almost certainly an incoming and/or an outgoing cargo door for river transport of trade goods. Postholes near and outside the door suggest that the cargo door opened onto a loading dock. Since the channel deep enough to carry merchant ships lay a quarter of a mile half mile offshore at that point on land, this likely functioned as a landing point for smaller craft to offload. Land that lay 1000 feet to the west was the only point where incoming ships could deliver their cargo without landing boats.[8]

We can determine when the warehouse was built by combining the historical archaeological record with datable stratified artifacts, in this case a single object (Figure 4.5). An extremely worn and purposely bent Charles I silver penny, minted ca. 1634–1635, was found buried in the building sub-floor which sets a definite *terminus post quem*, or a "date after which" the building stood.

It is difficult to estimate how long it took to wear the penny down to the condition it was in when someone apparently purposely bent and buried it. Wear, however, can serve as a general clue to when that might have happened. The shield on the coin is so worn it is almost unreadable, so one can reasonably guess that it circulated for a decade, from about 1635 to 1644. If so, it may be more than just a

FIGURE 4.4   Charred remains of warehouse basement wooden floor.

Source: Michael Lavin, JRF.

coincidence that 1644 was the year White patented the property and probably built his warehouse/house.

There could well be more to the meaning of this worn and bent penny than establishing the date of White's warehouse/house. First, it appears almost certain that someone folded the coin on purpose. Tradition has it that purposely folding a coin and then burying it was a cabalistic custom, one that rendered the coin capable of warding off evil spirits.[9] This custom appears to have been commonly practiced in early Jamestown. We found as many as 13 bent coins like this one deposited in early James Fort archaeological contexts. This coin is also not the only instance of deliberately buried but still useful objects found in earlier commercial buildings near the White warehouse. We found a square "case" bottle associated with citrine pebbles and an intact and still useable candle holder buried in the floor of the James Fort "factory" building just north of White's warehouse.[10] That building probably

FIGURE 4.5   Obverse and reverse bent 1634–1635 English penny found buried in the
warehouse basement floor shown with an unaltered parallel coin.

Source: Charles Durfor, JRF.

also served as a commercial building and a trading post. Trading jetton counters
were scattered across the factory floor.[11] One would almost have to conclude that
these unusual objects, the 1630s coin, the pebble bottle, and the candle holder, were
all signs that the Jamestown traders and merchants believed they would rid their
buildings of evil spirits. At least they probably hoped to do all they could to assure
themselves financial success.

White's warehouse does not represent the only remains of commercial buildings found in the east end of the developing Jamestown (Figure 4.6), It seems that
the area became a commercial district from the earliest years of the English settlement. National Park Service archaeologists found ruins of the first Jamestown
brewery and part of another warehouse building, the former along the Pitch and Tar
swamp directly north of the White warehouse and the latter built into the original

FIGURE 4.6   Shore location of White's warehouse/house and the building foundation on the original James River bank, probably the footing of a warehouse uncovered in 1936.

Source: May, JRF, National Park Service.

riverbank 200 feet to the east. We found a deposit of washed sand resting on jumbled trash dating to the second quarter of the seventeenth century between the White warehouse cargo door and the current river shore. Those deposits strongly suggest that the building stood right on the "original" river shore. The discovery of both warehouses on what appeared to be a sloping bank also indicated that, unlike the western end of Jamestown Island, the seventeenth-century shoreline has not eroded much at all since then.[12]

Historical archaeologists try, as much as possible, to physically reconstruct the material past which requires—along with the historical facts and artifacts—a certain flavor of logical imagination. The White warehouse ruin is no exception, even given its only partial archaeological footprint. We can get hints of the superstructure. Buildings as massive as White's, with its substantial chimneys and tile roof, suggest that the upper floor or floors were upscale domestic spaces: hence a warehouse/house. That was common in England. Good examples of dual-purpose warehouses still stand in Ipswich and Suffolk, the seaport frequented by the 1607 Jamestown leader Captain Bartholomew Gosnold. More such buildings still stand at the English seaport of King's Lynn, Norfolk, where Captain John Smith held a brief apprenticeship. These buildings also doubled as the merchant's houses conveniently located near the water's edge and easily accessible for cargo ships.

The unusual size of the White foundation also suggests that the superstructure had to be heavy enough to support a fairly elaborate roof framing, which probably would include double gables like the sixteenth-century customs house in the English river port town of Topsham. The Dutch Vingboons map of Jamestown Island seems to depict a multiple-gabled building located some distance from the western end of the island. This location appears to be on White's property, but his chimney locations only make architectural sense with a double—and not a triple—gable roof. That discrepancy seems to indicate that Vingboons only showed a representative icon for a fort and did not depict architectural detail. It may also have been drawn 27 years before White's 1644 land patent.

Nonetheless, with more fact and a little logical imagination, one can even generate some idea of the floor plan of the upper stories as well. Excavations uncovered the base of a key burned timber post located dead center in the building foundation. This post likely supported a central beam in the basement ceiling, which in turn supported timber walls dividing the spaces above into at least two rooms and most likely four on each floor. Further, fragments of wall plaster found on the burned floor boards must mean that, regardless of how many rooms stood above the cargo basement, these rooms were finely finished living spaces.

So, what caused the fire? An accidental burning is certainly possible but, as we have seen, White's house was not one of the "slight cottages" described by Governor Harvey. Those shelters had fire-prone wooden chimneys and thatched roofs. Given that White's building was heavily timber framed yet had brick chimneys and a tile roof, the chances of an accidental fire appear minimal. The cause of the fire could well have been arson. Was it purposely destroyed during a Virginia insurrection, possibly Bacon's Rebellion? A nearby burned house almost certainly was.

Notes

1 Sir William Berkeley, *A Discourse and View of Virginia* (1663), Warren Billings, *Sir William Berkeley Dictionary of Virginia Biography* (Richmond, VA) and Frank E. Grizzard, Jr., and Daniel Boyd Smith, *Jamestown Colony, A Political, Social, and Cultural History* (Santa Barbara, CA: ABC-CLIO, Inc., 2007), 223.
2 Jamestown Land Patents, Book 2, 10–11.
3 H. McIlwane. *Journals of the House of Burgess: 1619–1659* (London, 2018), 20; William Byrd, *Title Book: 1637–1743* (Virginia Historical Society); British Public Record Office, High Court of the Admiralty, I.
4 Much of the detailed references to the remains of this building are in: Eric Deetz, Carter C. Hudgins, Jamie May, Luke Pecoraro, Toni Rock, Daniel Schmidt, Beverly Shaube, 2000–2002 Interim Report, Jamestown Rediscovery Archaeological Project, 71–81.
5 Author, "Virginia under John Harvey," Virginia Magazine of History and Biography, III (1895), 29.
6 Eric Deetz in Jamestown Rediscovery Technical Report 2000–2006, p. 80.
7 John L. Cotter, *Archeological Excavations at Jamestown Virginia* (Washington, DC: National Park Service, 1958), 49.
8 The only landing point for off-loading ships close enough to the channel was 1200 west of the John White landing, the place where the first settlers could moor their ships to the trees. This became known as Church Point, which eroded away by ca. 1870. See Chapter 8.
9 Michael Shutty Jr., Bent, Holed and Folded (Shelbyville, KY: Wasteland Press, 2019), passim.
10 It was thought that citrine attracts wealth, prosperity, and success.
11 See William M. Kelso, Jamestown, the Buried Truth (Charlottesville: University of Virginia Press, 2006), 104.
12 Op. cit. Cotter, Archaeological Excavations, 63–65.

5

INSURRECTION

Jamestown was burned to the ground on July 30, 1676. That day, a frontier planter, Nathaniel Bacon, and hundreds of his supporters set the town ablaze. This insurrection became known as Bacon's rebellion.

Historians to this day debate about the motives of the rebels. However, most agree that one major cause of the rebellion and the burning of the capital city stemmed from the fact that the government, led by Governor William Berkeley, had passed laws that the rebels felt were keeping them from profiting from land development on western frontier. Berkeley forbade hinterland settlement where Bacon and other settlers had forcefully taken Indian land. Then Berkeley failed to spend tax money on defending them when the Indians retaliated. Consequently, Bacon and his followers marched on Jamestown to demand government protection from Indian raids, title to more of these western lands, and to abolish "unfair" taxes. Governor Berkeley's answer to these demands was to brand Bacon and his followers "rebels" who, at that time, promptly left town.

Consequently, a furious Bacon returned with a band of heavily armed frontiersman and threatened to shoot Berkeley as he stood on the steps of the Statehouse. Berkley answered with a shout: "Here shoot me before God." Bacon did not fire, but soon a thousand of his followers took up arms against Berkeley. They attacked the frontier Indians and besieged the General Assembly at Jamestown. This plunged Virginia into a disastrous civil war. During the revolt, Jamestown was captured and recaptured until Rebels finally burned it to the ground. All the public buildings and "twelve new brick houses and a considerable number of frame houses with brick chimneys" all went up in smoke.[1] Certainly, warehouses like John White's, if it was still standing, would have been prime targets for arson which would have aided in crippling the tobacco-based Virginia economy.[2]

DOI: 10.4324/9781003441670-5

Two of Nathaniel Bacon's staunchest Jamestown supporters were William Drummond and Richard Lawrence. Drummond was the former Governor of Carolina who was a man thoroughly disliked by Berkeley, and Lawrence was an assemblyman and Jamestown innkeeper. They both built houses close to each other near the Jamestown church in the 1660s and they both fought with Bacon as he burned and pillaged not only Jamestown but scores of Virginia plantations. During the torching of the town, both Drummond and Lawrence made a dramatic show of support for the rebellion by burning their own Jamestown houses and Lawrence was said to have set the Jamestown church and Statehouse afire himself.[3]

In the ensuing months, Bacon died of dysentery and soon the rebellion collapsed. Berkeley arrested Drummond and, without a trial, condemned him to death. He was hanged at Middle Plantation (future Williamsburg) on January 20, 1677. Lawrence fled Jamestown after the fire leaving behind "a cupboard full of plate" (silver?). Governor Berkeley officially accused him of high crimes and treason, which meant that he could not be pardoned. He was never arrested and he basically vanished from the records, allegedly dying in the snow.

Drummond likely built his Jamestown house that he would burn down, on the land near the church that Drummond's wife, Sarah, inherited from her first husband, mariner Edward Prescott.[4] The burned house remnants were found on Sarah's land so this was likely the site of Drummond's townhouse[5] (Figure 5.1).

The burned architectural remains and dates of artifacts found associated with the ruin do suggest that we had found the house that Drummond torched. Its remains consisted of a brick cellar, a brick chimney foundation, a fragmented chimney, and part of a foundation wall. At the time of that discovery, we were pursuing our major archaeological project goal: finding and interpreting the early archaeological remnants of James Fort. But the archaeological remains of this burned building appeared to be "masking" the sites of an early Fort period armorer's shop and main storehouse.[6] Again, this was a complicated archaeological situation because in order to uncover the Fort some non-Fort archaeological remains had to be uncovered, recorded, and "dismantled" to expose and interpret the earlier Fort remains. In the process of our digging, discovery of enough original fabric of the later house made it possible to conjecturally reconstruct it and to envision its ill-fated demise during Bacon's lost cause.

Archaeology is basically all about pattern recognition. In this case, sensing the spacial pattern of the fragmented parts of the burned house suggested what elements of the building were left intact and what parts of the foundation had not survived. In other words, despite the fact that we learned that most of the foundation had been plowed away in the nineteenth century, enough of the disarticulated brickwork survived to paste together a complete overall house ground plan. How so? Both remnants were aligned and on the same compass orientation as the cellar. That relationship made it almost certain that they were parts of the same 40′ x 20′ building. Moreover, destruction debris at the center of the western end of the cellar included brick paving tiles, almost certainly parts of a collapsed hearth, evidence that two exterior chimneys flanked the house. The tiles were found sealed

FIGURE 5.1 The Jamestown Rediscovery team and the Drummond House excavation with the Jamestown church in the background.

Source: Michael Lavin, JRF.

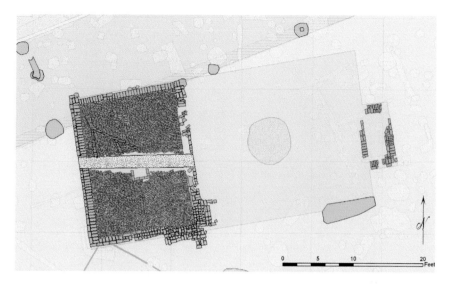

FIGURE 5.2 The archeological plan of the Drummond House.

Source: Jamie May.

by charcoal and ash from the fire suggesting that they fell through the floor as the building burned.

These architectural elements of the Drummond ruin suggested to us that the structure was likely a typical colonial house: a story and a half-frame building with exterior end chimneys and a two-room hall/parlor plan on either side of a central "passage" (Figure 5.3). That may seem to draw way too much from the minimal surviving elements of the building. But our hypothetical model of the pre-fire house is based on more than the uncovered architectural elements. Even though eyewitness documents describing this structure are basically non-existent (except that reference to Drummond's house being "the finest in town"), there are certain records of many houses in Virginia and Maryland typically built in the second half of the seventeenth century on through the eighteenth century that if they burned would leave an archaeological footprint similar to what we found on the Drummond site. In fact, these houses were so common they were collectively called "the Virginia House."[7] The larger examples were usually exactly like our Drummond House in plan, 20′ x 40′, have exterior end chimneys, have basements under part or all of the house, and were a story-and-one-half in height with a two-room hall/a parlor passage ground floor plan. The halls were the general-purpose public room and sometime earlier kitchens, while the parlor (or chamber) was more of a private space, often used as a bedroom. A steeply pitched roof provided space for a loft room or rooms. The stair to the half story would be located in the hall.

But **when** the Drummond House was built and **when** it burned are key questions to answer in order to determine the role it played in Jamestown history. As luck would

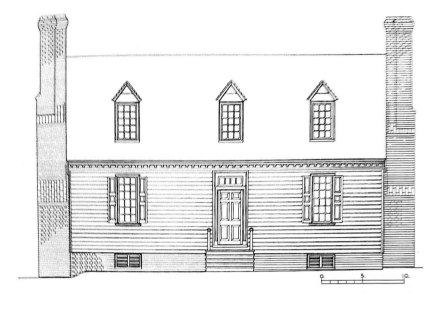

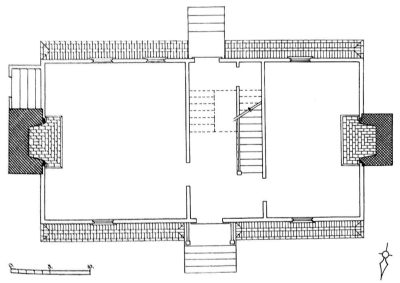

FIGURE 5.3   The Drummond House architectural remains are almost identical to the foundation plan of this Virginia House, the Bracken House, located on Francis Street in Colonial Williamsburg.

Source: Markus Whiffen, Colonial Williamsburg Foundation.

FIGURE 5.4   Obverse and reverse of a 1656 French Laird found in the Drummond House builder's trench.

Source: Michael Lavin, JRF.

have it, just like the White warehouse, a coin recovered from the ruins likely provided the answers. A 1656 French Laird was found in a collapsed section of what appeared to be fill in a trench dug when the builders laid the foundation wall of the cellar (the "builder's trench") (Figure 5.4). Ostensibly, this find once again establishes the year (1656) after which the building was built. A closer look at the displaced builder's trench fill, however, left some doubt that the coin wound up in that deposit at the time of construction but rather it got there during the time when the abandoned burned house basement was filled in. Of course, interpreting those nuances of strata is an essential challenge in historical archaeology. On the one hand, if the coin did drop into the trench during construction, then we could be confident that the building was built sometime after 1656. On the other hand, if the coin happened to fall into a "collapsed" builder's trench soil, then it likely wound up there **after** the house was destroyed by fire. So from its stratigraphic context, how soon after 1656 the coin wound up in the trench appears impossible to establish with perfect confidence.

Like White's apparent "magic" penny, however, there is another clue to chronology, the circulation wear. The Laird did appear worn to some extent, but way less than Whites' penny. Coupled with the slight wear, there appears to be documentary evidence that could define the circulation period fairly precisely. First of all, the building **does not** conform to a 1662 Jamestown legislative mandate, which explicitly stipulated

> That the towne to be built shall consist of thirty two houses, each house to be built with brick, forty foot long, twenty foot wide, within the walls, to be eighteen foote high above the ground, the walls to be two bricks thick to the water table, … the roofe to be fifteen foote pitch and to be covered with slate or tile.[8]

Obviously, our burned house did not comply with this law; it was not all brick and no slate or tile were found in the house destruction archaeological deposits. Still, it did meet the required overall size, 20' x 40'. So being a wooden structure, it was probably not a "compliance" house and therefore while probably built after the coin date 1656 it could have been built before the 1662 legislation. And if it was built, say, in 1661, then that five-year period circulation period could well have resulted in the slight wear condition of the Laird. But still, there is that pesky archaeological caveat to this conclusion, the uncertain context of the worn 1656 coin which could rule it out as a construction indicator after all. Still, if the coin did get into the builder's during construction yet after the brick house law went into effect, who is to say that Drummond was not already disregarding laws a decade before they illegally aimed their muskets at Governor Berkeley? Furthermore, Drummond had his mansion, Greenspring, on his plantation nearby on the mainland so why would he build an expensive brick house in the town that, as a Burgess, he may have only needed when the General Assembly was in session. In any case, we can conclude that the burned house was almost certainly standing by 1676 and likely burned by Drummond on September 20, 1676 when the rebels went about incinerating the entire town. And they did a thorough job of it. References indicate that they made sure there was not a habitable structure left in the town and for "five miles around" when the victorious Berkeley forces arrived in Virginia looking for shelter.[9]

There are many more architectural details to be gleaned from the archaeological remnants of the burned house. We found two sets of brick stairs leading down into the brick basement from two different directions (Figure 5.5). One, the narrowest, leads from inside the house and the other wider stairs lead from outside of the south side of the house. They were likely two different sizes for good reason. The larger was a "bulkhead" entrance which would typically open onto the "street." Bulkheads were used to facilitate deliveries of bulky barrels or boxes. So it follows that the other narrower basement stairs would likely be only intended for pedestrian use, probably accessed from under passage steps by servants or slaves to get to and from what was almost certainly, at least in part, the wine storage cellar.

Just like the other James Fort buildings found archaeologically, the abandoned Drummond House cellar was ultimately filled with plowed dirt above a deposit of garbage and trash. Just below that overburden we found only discarded broken bricks again likely discarded by salvagers going after reusable bricks. Below that lay a deposit of the ashen building remains which in turn rested on the intact brick floor. Much of the charred fabric of the building wound up *in situ* in the ash layer: a heavy layer of burned timbers, fallen plaster, roof and hearth tiles laying among burned barrels, and other artifacts dating to the second half of the seventeenth century (Figure 5.6). So this deposit was almost certainly fallout from the fire that destroyed the wood-framed house above, a tightly dated archaeological time capsule deposited in the cellar on the Bacon's fire day, September 19, 1676.

FIGURE 5.5 Exterior (right) and interior (left) cellar stairs.

Source: Michael Lavin, JRF.

The basement deposit held more clues to the fabric of the house. We found fragments of wall plaster adhered to the underside some of the burned timbers indicating that these were framing members from a "finished" room above. We also found the charred remains of six upright casks, two bucket bottoms, and a small wooden box with an iron lock. Of course, the barrels could have been used to store wine. But because they were burned as they stood upright, they were probably empty at the time of the fire; filled wine casks were generally stored on their sides for tapping. The diameters of the burned casks indicated that when they were full they could have once held 550 liters or one "pipe" of wine, a valuable commodity. While Drummond or Lawrence may have wisely removed other full wine barrels before torching their own houses, other townsmen were not so wise. Sixty-three pipes of wine elsewhere in town did go up in flames.[10] Also dense nail concentrations were found scattered across the basement floor, not unexpected finds on the site of a burned frame building. Other building parts and some furniture hardware found in the burned layer included a door key, a door lock with its key, a pintle for a window shutter hinge, a charred copper-alloy keyhole escutcheon from a chest, and an iron cabinet hinge. We were tempted to conclude that these objects were being used as hardware and furnishings in the rooms above and then fell into the basement as doors, windows, and furniture burned away. If that did happen, then their exact resting place on the basement floor would likely be clues to more architectural details and furnishings of the house at the time of the fire. However, if they

FIGURE 5.6   Charred wooden remains of framing timbers and barrels on the Drummond cellar floor.

Source: Michael Lavin, JRF.

did fall directly from the burned rooms above, one would expect to find **pairs** of door hinges, much window glass, window lead, iron casement window frames, and many furniture fittings as well. They were not there. That suggests two scenarios: the house either was empty and stripped of doors and windows before the fire or salvagers recovered some of these items from the ash as they collected the intact bricks. But it is important to note that it appeared that some of what remained of the ash level on the basement floor did not appear to have been sifted through by anyone looking for reusable non-combustibles. This could indeed mean, like the probable missing wine, that Drummond stripped down and emptied the house before he burned it. This seems to say that Drummond may have had limits on how much of his own portable possessions he would sacrifice for Bacon's cause. To destroy a common frame Virginia House was one thing but the expensive glass in metal casement windows, door hardware, and furniture were quite another. Consequently, the lack of evidence of these things in the ash may offer insight into the mindset of at least one of the rebels. It may be that Drummond did squirrel away materials for house rebuilding at some future time. As it turned out, of course, his death soon after the revolt literally "killed" that plan.

Other artifacts found among the burned debris are datable to the last third of the seventeenth century (Figure 5.7). These objects were probably discards left

FIGURE 5.7   Restored German Bartman jug that had exploded during the Drummond House fire.

Source: Michael Lavin, JRF.

by someone who had worked in the basement at that time and not things that fell in from rooms above as a result of the fire. The finds included a charred German stoneware jug exploded by the heat, a type commonly made in the period ca. 1650–1680. It was possibly intended to become a wine decanter. A trumpet-shaped brass candlestick base, a fire-molten square case bottle glass, and burned tobacco pipe fragments were also found in the ash. One pipe bore the initials "WP" likely identifying the English pipe maker, William Evans. According to record, he made pipes in London in the period ca. 1660–1682. Another pipe bowl we found in the ash had a stylistic bowl shape common to the period ca. 1660–1680.[11] Three fragments of jewelry were also found on the floor: two sections of twisted silver wire and a square cut jewel in a gold setting. Could these have been dropped there by a jeweler making repairs?

Another artifact found in the ash layer may reflect directly on the cause and makeup of Bacon's "Choice and Standing Army." An iron shackle, either a horse restraining device known as a "hobble" or possibly part of a slave's leg iron, was found lying in the ash at the base of the narrow interior basement stair (Figure 5.8). Was this an ankle shackle broken by the rebels to add a liberated slave to their pyrotechnic army? Probably not. But ten percent of Bacon's forces were enslaved people that he freed or were former slaves who had already gained their freedom. In fact, "Of the last one hundred holdouts among the Baconian headquarters guard, eighty were black."[12]

Little wonder that they were loyal to the rebel cause until the end; they had the most to gain if the rebellion succeeded and the most to lose if it failed. And lose they did. In the end, the "80," and most of the revolution's black soldiers, were returned to slavery, even in instances where they had been promised their freedom as the price of laying down their arms. And this treatment was true even for already free African-American planters. For example, a "Mulatto," Edward Lloyd, and his wife were free blacks before the rebellion and they stayed neutral in the rebellion as much as they could in order "… to preserve their hard won property and status." But to no avail; they too were enslaved again after the rebellion.[13]

In the end, white leaders like Drummond paid the ultimate price for backing Bacon. Twenty-three were hanged, most of them without a trial, and many were executed "… in their countryside," (where they lived) so their friends could witness their deaths as a lesson to henceforth abide by the Governor's strict rules. Of course, Jamestown was Drummond's "countryside." But the ruinous town was evidently abandoned and therefore unable to gather the compulsory crowd to view his execution. So that is probably why Middle Plantation (Williamsburg) located nine miles northeast of Jamestown was the substitute hanging site for Drummond.

The burned ruins reflected more about the house. They appeared to show that the masons were not the most skilled but they did have enough of the best bricks. All the bricks were of uniform size suggesting a well-planned and supplied building project. Still, apparently the supply ran short at some point. So the south cellar wall, a rather roughly built footing made of cobbles and heavy mortar, and the east wall were based on a structurally weak footing made up of mixture of broken roofing tiles, cobbles,

FIGURE 5.8 Iron shackle or horse hobble found on the interior steps of the Drummond House cellar.

Source: Michael Lavin, JRF.

and brickbats. To be fair, however, the masons could get by with this haphazardly built wall since it only had to support the weight of one passage wall above. The masons did however build a sump in the basement floor and slanted the floor to drain into it. This probably indicates that the workmen had learned the lesson of building basements, even shallow English basements, below or near to the shallow Virginia ground water table. So one could also conclude that they were native-born Virginians or seasoned immigrants since they knew the local ground water problem.

After considering the countless archaeological details of the burned White warehouse and Drummond House and the chances that they were torched by Bacon's rebels, one might reasonably ask: "What has the discovery and analysis of these burned buildings sites added to what were already known about the Bacon's rebellion story?" That is, how much more can we understand about the event now that we have physical evidence of it? The burning of the warehouse, a fundamental cog in the Tobacco economy upon which so many Virginians livelihood depended, and the burned town house certainly reflect how seriously committed men like Drummond were to upending the status quo. These burned ruins also point out that modern acts of arson fueled by mass political protest is nothing new in the American experience.[14]

We found that the Drummond House remains were not the only Post-Fort period building with a filled brick-lined cellar (Figure 5.9 and 5.10). While removing the plowzone soil southwest of the burned ruin, much to our surprise, we found a small roughly brick-lined cellar built "through" a section of the 1610 Governor's Rowhouse chimney foundation. Both the chimney footing of the earlier building and the cellar foundation became visible at the same level under the plowzone. Consequently, we could not determine which "came first" in time just from the relative context. However, the two foundations had been built at an angle to each other which was a telling horizontal clue to chronology. How so? Simply this; structures from the same period are invariably aligned or they are built using the same compass orientation. So the mis-alignment of the two structures and the fact that the cellar cut into the earlier chimney foundation meant that it was constructed after the Row chimney was built and likely after 1624, when the Governors moved to new houses northeast of the Fort.

Just like the other Post-Fort period archeological building remains, there was much to learn from the actual excavation of the fill in this cellar and the features surrounding it. The basically intact basement walls indicated that it was 22′ across but only 8′ wide. Being that narrow it was likely only under part of an above-ground structure. It was also clear that there was evidence that the structure above it had been a post-in-the-ground timber building. Three structural postholes were found along the south basement wall, one at each corner and one at the center. The south brick wall was laid **against** these once standing posts so the cellar had to have been built under a standing post-building. And two more aligned postholes were found 18′ south of the basement apparently making the overall size of the structure only 22′ x 24′. There was no evidence of a hearth but it is likely that if it had ever existed plowing had erased any signs of it.

FIGURE 5.9 Brick-lined late seventeenth-century cellar found superimposed on the chimney foundation of the James Fort Governor's Row.

Source: Michael Lavin, JRF.

FIGURE 5.10   A cache of late seventeenth-century wine bottles found on the floor of the
small cellar building.

Source: Michael Lavin, JRF.

This was a very small outbuilding suggesting that it was a kitchen or a slave quarter. If it was a kitchen, then one would expect to have found a main house nearby aligned with it. This was not the case at least in the area we exposed previously to the west. Seventeenth-century kitchens were usually in the halls or the basements of the main houses and it was not generally until the late seventeenth to eighteenth century that they were relegated to outbuildings, about the same time enslaved Africans come into Virginia in any numbers. In fact, from 1677 to 1700 the enslaved population had quadrupled from 2000 to 8000.[15] So if the tiny cellar building was occupied during the late seventeenth century, the chances are it was built for and by enslaved people. There is more telling evidence for that conclusion.

First, the dates of artifacts found sealed beneath the building rubble and on the basement floor together date the lifespan of the building with unusual accuracy to the very late seventeenth to the early eighteenth century. Ten intact glass wine bottles of a shape common in the period 1680–1700 were left on the original floor. One bore a seal with the initials "FN," "FN" almost certainly indicating that this bottle was made for and once owned by Sir Francis Nicholson who served as Virginia's lieutenant governor from 1690 to 1692 and governor from 1698 to 1705. Nicholson did live in rental property at Jamestown while his permanent residence, the "Governor's Palace," was under construction in Williamsburg. Secondly, we found pieces of dated and "signed" stripes of lead from casement windows on the floor of the cellar as well. One of the 17 window strips was impressed with the initials and manufacture date: "E.W*1693*W.C*." This established, with an unusual degree of certainty, the date after which the cellar was in use (the TPQ). So again, the artifacts recovered from the cellar fill almost certainly date it to the last decade of the seventeenth century when slavery became common.

Thirdly, more telling of the occupants of the building is the **types** of artifacts left in the cellar. Along with common 1660–1690 European tobacco pipe bowls, two iron stirrups, an iron spit, a hoe blade, and a gun barrel were in the fill. These are objects of some value suggesting that this cellar was a "safe," where slaves salted away objects hidden from the eyes of the master. (Figure 5.11) The intact bottles, especially the Nicholson bottle, and the iron objects could have been intended for bartering, traded later for whatever the slaves needed beyond what the slave owner

FIGURE 5.11   The types of artifacts found in the brick-lined "root cellar" conform with a pattern of object collections found archaeologically in cellars on hundreds of Virginia and Maryland plantation slave quarter sites.

Source: Archaearium exhibit, JRF.

would supply. This interpretation might seem beyond the singular Jamestown evidence. It is not. I have personally found literally dozens of cellars containing intact wine bottles with owner's seals and useable iron tools and implements on colonial slave quarters sites. Hundreds more plantation sites found in Virginia and Maryland reflect the same pattern.[16] It follows that this Jamestown house with its cellar clandestinely full of "hidden" objects is one of the earliest slave quarters yet found in Colonial America.

Notes

1 John Davenport Neville, *Bacon's Rebellion Abstracts of Materials in the Public Records Project* (Jamestown, ND: Jamestown Foundation), 267.
2 No artifacts found associated with the building dated as late as 1676.
3 M. McCartney, *Jamestown Archaeological Assessment, II* (Williamsburg, VA, 1998), 46.
4 Ibid. 145, 250–251.
5 The precise location of Sarah's inherited land is somewhat speculative.
6 Op. cit. Kelso. Buried Truth, 243.
7 Marcus Whiffen, *The Eighteenth Century Houses of Williamsburg* (The Colonial Williamsburg Foundation, 1960), 67.
8 William Waller Henning, *Statutes at Large* (1823), 172.
9 Op. cit. Neville, *Bacon's Rebellion*, 310.
10 Ibid. ("Personal Grievances of Certain Inhabitants of Virginia Sworn Before the Commissioners", July 1677, 371).
11 Ivor Noel Hume, *A Guide to the Artifacts of Colonial America* (New York, 1970), 303.
12 Stephan Saunders Webb, *1676 The End of American Independence* (Syracuse, NY, 1996), 6.
13 Ibid. 454.
14 Forces, *Tracts* (1896), 1:8:21.
15 Op. cit. Neville, Bacon's Rebellion, passim.
16 William M. Kelso, (San Diego: Academic Press, 1984), 119–128. Patricia M. Sanford, *Subfloor Pits and the Archaeology of Slavery in Colonial Virginia* (Tuscaloosa: The University of Alabama Press, 2007). Sanford makes a case that the arrangement of some of these objects on the "pit" floors constitutes a traditional African shrine rather than a "hidey-hole" for future trade behind the owner's back. While that interpretation is possible, I do not think it is probable.

6

THE STATEHOUSE

During the initial construction of a Jamestown concrete seawall by the Corps of Engineers in 1901, the engineer in charge, Samuel Yonge, discovered a brick building foundation protruding from the eroded river bank along the western end of the APVA's property. He then proceeded to dig into the ruins. In his book, *The Site of Old Jamestown, 1903*, he made record of the foundations he traced. He uncovered the entire extent of the brickwork by digging along the walls that revealed the remains of five contiguous buildings built over time from the riverside eastward. He also found the foundations of six chimneys and two additions with cellars to the north. He concluded from the melted lead he found in the cellar and from historical accounts that the building had been attacked and burned by Bacon's rebels. Yonge also concluded that the plan of easternmost unit of the five-part building complex fit documentary references to the place where the Virginia legislature met. While the excavation was crude by modern standards, his work was remarkably thorough and his interpretations insightful. Besides the melted lead, Yonge recovered a number of other artifacts from the fill in the cellars. There he found iron hinges and a distinctive type of door lock, a number of military items including exploded hand grenades, bill hooks (pole arms), and cannon balls—more evidence of Bacon's fire. At the conclusion of his dig, as an exhibit, the complex of foundations were marked with concrete caps at ground level.[1]

As a contribution to the 350th celebration of Jamestown's founding, the APVA and the National Park Service considered reconstruction of the easternmost unit of the Statehouse Complex that Yonge identified as the "third and fourth State House." This goal spawned two major archaeological studies of the eastern end unit of the complex, the statehouse, led by National Park Service archaeologists. Their first statehouse excavation in 1952 found a partition wall foundation undetected by Yonge, burned floor joists, some roofing tiles, and slate.

DOI: 10.4324/9781003441670-6

FIGURE 6.1   When he was directing the construction of a seawall to protect the Jamestown shoreline, Samuel Yonge (left) discovered and then partially excavated (right) the eroding "third ridge" foundations of the seventeenth-century Statehouse Complex.

Source: JRF, APVA.

A number of artifacts were found amid the building ruins, including leads from casement-type windows bearing dates of 1678, 1683, and 1686. The archaeologists concluded that these were lost during the rebuilding of the complex after the Bacon's Rebellion fire. They also speculated that the site served as a burial ground during Jamestown's 1609–1610 "starving time."[2]

As plans for 2007 commemoration of the founding of Jamestown jelled, the planners decided to build a modern museum building directly on the Statehouse Complex site. Consequently, Jamestown Rediscovery archaeologists conducted yet another excavation of the complex site, but this time their purpose was to mitigate any impact that the museum construction would have on the seventeenth-century structural remains of the statehouse and the burials. The results of that work further refined Yonge's sequencing of the construction of the various statehouse building units through time by defining certain masonry and frame details from unit to unit. A combination of archaeology, records searches, and an architectural survey of brick English and American buildings produced a conjectural reconstruction of the complex.[3]

We confirmed Yonge's conclusion based on abutting brick foundations of the contiguous buildings (Figure 6.5_). The five of them were indeed built from west to east through time. We not-so-creatively named them buildings 1-2, 3-4, 5.[4]

FIGURE 6.2   Exploded hand grenades and bill hook blades from the early Statehouse Yonge excavations (JRF).

We also found more evidence to back up the relative construction sequence. For example, we found that the mortar used to bond the brick foundations of the two double units was identical—suggesting that they were built around the same time. Next, we agreed with Yonge that houses 1 and 2 were doubled in size and cellars added, but concluded that whether this happened before or after house 5 existed at the eastern end of the line of buildings was not evident. No artifacts excavated in 1903 can be reliably ascribed to deposition during construction, so a precise time for the addition remains unknown. The relatively scant fragments of builder's fill that survived the 1950s excavations along the Building 5 foundation also produced nothing datable. A preponderance of "early style" flat clay roofing tiles on the site

FIGURE 6.3 Window lead from the 1956 National Park Service excavation, dated 1678, 1683, and 1686.

Source: Michael Lavin, JRF.

of Buildings 1 and 2, however, and an apparent shift to "later style" curved ceramic pantiles found amid the footings of Buildings 3 and 4, could be attributed to both the post-Bacon's Rebellion fire rebuild and a remodeling campaign. At that time, the more modern end stacks replaced old style central chimneys.

Yonge reported finding an additional "porch" foundation, which he proceeded to cap in concrete as he did all the other footings (Figure 6.6). Since its location—straddling the union of buildings 2 and 3—makes no logical architectural sense, this footing was not excavated further in 2002. No brick footing was found under the concrete. This is puzzling, because Yonge clearly understood the other footings. He guessed that this odd footing belonged to some earlier structure. The datable artifacts from this so-called footing, however, dated with unusual precision to the last third of the seventeenth century, including window leads of 1671 and 1686 and a tradesman's token from London's Globe Tavern dated 1667.

Documentary records left little doubt how the buildings of the Statehouse Complex came to be, what function they served, and, in particular, which of them was the Statehouse itself. In 1662, King Charles II charged the restored Governor Berkeley with a renewed and more serious effort to develop Jamestown into the prototypical "Cittie" it was "supposed to be." Berkeley determined the building's specifications, which included a number of brick houses of standard size built at a scale that would command the respect of the Crown, as well as prominence and permanence for the colony. In all likelihood this legislation resulted in construction

FIGURE 6.4 An in-depth architectural study produced a conjectural reconstruction of the entire Statehouse Complex.

Source: Cary Carson (Carl Lounsbury, JRF).

of the earliest four of the westernmost units of the Statehouse Complex. Building 5 the meeting place of the colonial government was completed by 1665: "[we have] begun a town of brick & have already built enough to accommodate both ye public affairs of ye country."[5]

By the 1670s, the four westernmost houses were leased primarily for government use or for the use of Berkeley's political friends. Building 1 was the "country's house" that served as Berkeley's town apartment. Next to the "country's house" a Major Theophilus Hone lived while he built a brick "fort" near the

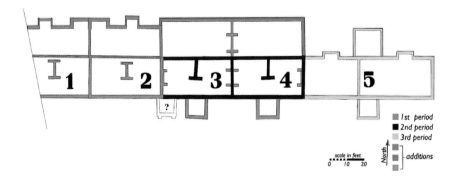

FIGURE 6.5 Plan of Statehouse Complex excavations, 2002, showing the Brick footings sequence: Building 3-4 built onto and therefore after Building 1-2, the non-bonded footings between 3-4 and 5, and the two rear additions.

Source: Jamie May, JRF.

south end of the complex. After Bacon's rebels destroyed the wooden interiors of the entire Statehouse complex, Hone successfully petitioned the Assembly for a 50-year lease of the ruins of Buildings 3 and 4, which required him to rebuild them. He evidently never did. At the same time, Colonel Philip Ludwell petitioned for a lease for Buildings 3 and 4, and a contiguous acre and a half of land. But just as Hone did not rebuild Buildings 1 and 2, Ludwell failed to rebuild Buildings 3 and 4. Eventually, Buildings 2, 3, and 4 passed to Ludwell's

FIGURE 6.6 Globe Tavern London trade token 1667 from the fill inside Yonge's mystery "porch foundation."

Source: Jamie May, JRF.

son, Philip Ludwell II. Then, on April 20, 1694, Ludwell II received a grant from Governor Edmond Andros for one and a half acres of land to adjoin his buildings.

The parcel's width—124 feet—is exactly that of the width of the foundations of Buildings 2, 3, and 4, so this grant also confirms that Building 1 was still a "country's house," ostensibly for the governor.

It seems logical that since Ludwell owned Buildings 2, 3, and 4 and the one and a half acres of land adjoining them, he likely would have been the person who rebuilt the entire complex. He doubled it in size and did the "modernization "of the floor plan of the ruins of Buildings 3 and 4. This effort included moving the kitchen to the north addition, replacing the old-fashioned central H-shaped fireplaces with the end chimneys, and adding porch tower entries to replace the old-fashioned lobby entrances. Within six years, however, all this renovation proved for naught. It took a 1698 fire, and not Nathaniel Bacon, to erase Ludwell's townhouse and the appended Statehouse Complex for good. Quite unexpectedly though, our archaeological story of the Statehouse Complex and Philip Ludwell II did not end with our study of his leveled townhouse. A serendipitous discovery in the Jamestown churchyard gave us a unique opportunity to literally come face to face with Ludwell himself. It happened this way:

In 2012, Mr. William Harrison, a 12th-generation Harrison, visited the Jamestown churchyard and read on an APVA interpretive plaque that one of the gravestones marked the burial place of early settler Benjamin Harrison. He also soon learned from us that the stone, which had no epitaph, was placed there to mark the grave where, in 1901, the APVA thought they had found the skeletal remains of his Harrison ancestor. They based their identification on copper tacks in the grave that they concluded once spelled out the name of the deceased. After a scrabble-like attempt at putting them back in order, they concluded that the tacks had originally been fastened to a coffin and spelled out "B. Harrison." At the conclusion of their dig, they then mended pieces of an unmarked gravestone and placed it on the grave. The copper tacks were salvaged and added to other sundry "finds" in the APVA archives.

Mr. Harrison contacted us and told us about his years-long quest to find the grave of his seventeenth-century Harrison relative. He was convinced that his quest to find the grave was now over. He had also searched for a portrait of Benjamin, to no avail, but he had read about our forensic study of other Jamestown skeletal remains that resulted in facial reconstructions. He told us that he wanted a re-excavation of the APVA-marked grave to recover the "Harrison remains" so that a forensic artist could recreate "B. Harrison's" facial appearance. And he would pay for it all. We saw this as a chance to not only find and study the remains of Benjamin Harrison or whoever lay beneath this unmarked mended gravestone but also to get a sense of the degree to which the APVA excavators had actually disturbed this and other graves they had uncovered in the adjacent church foundations and the churchyard in the 1890s. We did warn Mr. Harrison that there were a number of reasons why this grave was not necessarily B. Harrison's. First of all, we told him that the former interpretation of the largely scrambled tacks might not have spelled B. Harrison after all. Any skeletal remains found could have been those of an unknown person. And even if they were Harrison, we told Mr. Harrison that the bones might have been seriously damaged by the APVA dig or be extremely decayed, both or either of which would eliminate any possibility of forensic facial reconstruction. Nonetheless, Harrison still wanted to take a chance that our possible negative scenarios were wrong. Our two-month-long meticulous excavation began.

After removing the gravestone, we slowly inched into the grave fill to define the soil outline of the former APVA's digging. This initial excavation actually uncovered the outline of two graves. Then, to make things even more complex, removal of more of the upper grave fill revealed four episodes of past excavations: (1) the APVA dig, (2) a clear outline of a grave shaped like a hexagonal coffin, (3) a partially disturbed earlier grave of a teenaged girl, and (4) the disarticulated bones of a child. Finding these multi-burials and remains came as no surprise. The APVA digging had found what they described as "the skeletons of two grown persons and of at least one child."[6] They missed, however, the big surprise that was yet to come.[7] Once the earlier remains were recovered, our digging concentrated on the undisturbed part of the hexagonal grave—speculating that this would prove to be the resting place of "B. Harrison" (Figure 6.7). Indeed, digging deeper we uncovered a copper tack-lined wooden coffin, leading us to believe that this would be the Harrison found in 1901. A slow and painstaking exposure of the coffin lid (left primarily undisturbed in 1901), however, revealed a totally different message spelled out in the tacks. It read:

Phillip
Ludwell EsqR
DIED II JAN 1726 7
AGED 54
Yrs

To our great elation, this proved to be the grave of the aforementioned heir to the remodeled middle buildings of the Statehouse Complex: Philip Ludwell II, who, according to record, did die on January 11, 1726/27 at the age of 54. Knowing Ludwell's recorded death date and age helped us to fill in the missing tack letters amid the letters still in place.

Needless to say, Mr. Harrison was not happy, but we were ecstatic. We had not only found the ruins of Philip Ludwell's rebuilt Jamestown Statehouse townhouse to the west, but we had without a doubt found the remains of the man who occupied it whenever he had to be in town to serve as assemblyman and speaker of the house. Personalizing place-based history could not get any better than this.

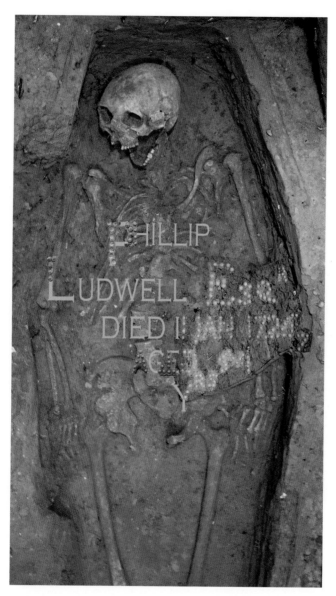

FIGURE 6.7   Epitaph of Philip Ludwell II spelled out in copper tacks on the remains of
his coffin with conjectural words and numbers.

Source: Michael Lavin, JRF.

FIGURE 6.8   A probable portrait of Philip Ludwell II.

Source: Robet E. Lee Memorial Association.

We were left, however, with explaining the tack letters allegedly spelling "B. Harrison" recovered by the APVA in 1901 from what we now knew was the grave of Philip Ludwell. Taking a closer look at the coffin wood grain adhering to the APVA tacks proved that they were never aligned to spell "B Harrison" at all. The APVA excavators had arranged the tacks to fit their documentary assumption that the elite Benjamin Harrison would have to have been buried in the prestigious Jamestown churchyard. We had also learned after the fact that embossing tacks on coffins, for decorative purposes or to spell out an epitaph of the deceased, was not used in English funerary practice until the eighteenth century.[8] Benjamin Harrison died in 1637, a century before the use of tack epitaphs became common. Despite the fact that the APVA tacks were allegedly found in Ludwell's grave, they likely wound up there because their digging had inadvertently partially dug into another later grave next door to the south.

Identifying Ludwell's grave erroneously as Harrison's also led to another significant APVA interpretive leap of faith. Scores of fragmented tombstones (ledgerstone?) were found during a 1901–1907 APVA cleanup of the ruinous church

Ruins of Jamestown.

FIGURE 6.9 The ruinous Jamestown churchyard as depicted in an 1854 drawing? A mystical engraving of the Jamestown tower ruin with broken gravestones in the foreground.

graveyard. They proceeded to piece them together, filling in missing letters or words in a process not unlike simultaneously working a giant jigsaw and crossword puzzle. One restoration attempt read:

> "Here lies interred the body of Phillip Ludwell who died the 11ᵗʰ of January in the 54ᵗʰ year of his age, sometime auditor of his Majesties revenue and twenty-five years a member of the Council". They placed it over a grave two burial spaces to the south of what we now know was his actual grave.

The APVA also found yet more fragmented ledgerstones in the abandoned and vandalized churchyard site. After a valiant effort to piece them together with helpful hints from an 1847 inventory taken by a Bishop Meade, at least 20 stones were "restored" and placed in line with the patched-together Ludwell stone. These marked the graves they had located with their digging across the site. That line and others made up a "restored" memorialized churchyard, complete with a map identifying as many as ten of the resting places of high-status Jamestown leaders and families. Number #13 read: "Benjamin Harrison." We now knew this was a mistake—mislabeling Ludwell's actual grave. Unfortunately, Mr. Harrison had taken the identification map as gospel. Who could blame him? Few people realize that seemingly infallible interpretations of the past are filled with educated guesses even though, in this case, they were cast in stone.

FIGURE 6.10   The ledgerstone of Philip Ludwell II found and pieced together during the early twentieth-century APVA "cleanup" of the Church graveyard.

Source: Author's courtesy.

Forensic analysis at the Smithsonian National Museum of Natural History adds more to what we learned from Ludwell's bones. There were no surprises for this upper-class person. He was 6′ tall, his *"... bones do not display developed muscle attachments and robusticity indicative of frequent heavy physical labor,"* there were tobacco pipe wear marks on his teeth, and he had lost his small right "pinky" finger. His teeth wear did suggest that he died in his 50s.[9]

Again, the last event in the chronicle of Jamestown statehouses and Philip Ludwell's house was yet another fire. This conflagration sealed Jamestown's fate as the former meeting place of Virginia's government in 1698. That function soon moved to nearby Williamsburg. The fire began in a building adjoining the statehouse section of the complex, Building 4's cellar addition, which seems to have become a prison. According to records, on October 20, 1698, "fire broke out in a house adjoining the State-house, which in a very short time was wholly burnt, and also the prison." This fire too appears to have been arson. Speculation suggests that one Arthur Jarvis set the fire. He had been sentenced to death for "Burglary & Felony," and probably locked up in the Statehouse Complex jail awaiting execution. Revenge may have been his motive. If Jarvis set the fire, however, he did it in such a way that the authorities could not prove it.[10]

The evolution of representative self-government at Jamestown in the seventeenth century, as reflected in the buildings and the individuals associated with it, is one of the most significant of Jamestown's stories. Archaeology has established that the 1665–1698 Statehouse Complex was in its day the largest secular public building in seventeenth-century America. With its two stories and garrets, additions, porch chambers, cellars, and a stair tower, the complex totaled 23,000 square feet under its roof. It can also be argued that what happened there held significance beyond the scope of government in the other colonies in the seventeenth century. Within the walls of the Jamestown Statehouse Complex, the legacy of the 1619 first representative assembly in North America evolved into a form of government that later day native sons Thomas Jefferson and George Washington would consider a birthright worth dying to preserve. Jamestown's governmental legacy is mixed. Within the walls of that Jamestown Capitol, the enslavement of Africans became rigid law and only a landed few men had the right to vote. At the same time, the mechanism to outlaw slavery and enfranchise a diverse country of the future grew from a process born in the statehouses at Jamestown. Such is the sacred and profane value of this Jamestown place of America's beginnings. Nathaniel Bacon could not burn that away.

Notes

1 Samuel H. Yonge, *The Site of Old "James Towne," 1607–1698* (Richmond, VA: The Association for the Preservation of Virginia antiquities, 1903), passim.
2 Louis R. Kaywood, *Report on the Excavations at the Site of the Third Ridge... MSS* (Colonial National Historic Park, 1954), Joel L. Shiner, *Report on the Excavation in the Area of the Statehouse... MSS* (Colonial National Historic Park, 1955).

3 Cary Carson, et al., Structure 144, MSS Report for the APVA, passim.
4 The discussion of the Jamestown Rediscovery Statehouse excavations that follows is gleaned from Jamie May, Report on the Statehouse Excavations, Jamestown Rediscovery Archives, and it is an abridged version of the Statehouse excavation discussed in Kelso, *The Buried Truth* (2006).
5 Warren Billings, *Sir William Berkeley* (Baton Rouge, 2004). ch.II.
6 Op. cit. Cotter, *Excavations at Jamestown*, 223.
7 Ibid.
8 Jullian Litton, *The English Way of Death* (London, 1992), 106.
9 Douglas Owsley, personal communication.
10 Wilson Noel Sainsbury, Calendar of State Papers, Colonial Series, 16:513, 516.

7

THE CHURCHES

Bacon's fire also failed to permanently erase the other symbol of the Jamestown establishment: the Brick Church. Like the brick statehouse complex, the fire reduced the building to a masonry shell that was also destined to be rebuilt. The fire only paused services—they were likely resumed by ca. 1680 and carried on until ca. 1750. After the mid-eighteenth century, the island church was succeeded by Burton Parish Church in Williamsburg and the Main Church nearby on the mainland. That is not the end of the Jamestown church story, however. Just like the archaeological research of the Statehouse Complex site, the early twentieth and twenty-first centuries' interest in uncovering the remains of burned Jamestown's "public" structures focused on the Jamestown church site.[1]

In 1902, the president of the Association for the Preservation of Virginia Antiquities (APVA), Mary Jeffery Gault, with Mary Garett and engineer John L. Tyler, ended their excavations of the church building foundations next to the iconic seventeenth-century church tower ruin (Figure 7.1).

They dug there because they knew that the first meeting of a democratic government in North America took place in the early timber church choir/chancel in 1619. The APVA excavators initially set out to learn whatever they could about that prophetic original timber structure. They also knew that the Timber Church only stood for 20 years before a Brick Church replaced it on the same site in 1647. The excavators also set out to study the remains of that brick replacement building before the Society of Colonial Dames of America built a Memorial Church to commemorate the 300th anniversary of the founding of "the American nation" in 1907.

Digging east of the tower, the APVA leaders and a number of laborers found sections of a brick-on-cobblestone foundation laying within a later brick foundation. They concluded that the cobble foundation was either the footing of a church built in 1608 or the foundation of the Timber Church that replaced it in 1617.

DOI: 10.4324/9781003441670-7

FIGURE 7.1 APVA excavation of the churches' site 1890–1902.

Source: APVA.

According to their reports, they also dug into a number of graves in the eastern end of the footings which had been the chancel of both churches. There they found two stone grave markers. One was a ledgerstone memorializing a Church Minister, Reverend Clough. It read: "Here lyeth interred the body of Rev. John Clough, late minister of this place, who departed this life January 15, 1683-4 and waits in hopes of a joyful resurrection."[2] Actually, Clough could have died eight years earlier, after he was captured by Bacon and condemned to death. He likely received a pardon, however, because he was a man of the cloth.[3]

The top of the other stone, made of black Belgian limestone, was found broken into pieces, which probably happened when a heavy roof timber fell on it either during Bacon's fire or when the roof or the brick superstructure collapsed on it in the second half of the eighteenth century. (Figure 7.2) Despite the breaks in the Belgian stone, the APVA excavators saw recessed impressions (known as indents) where brass memorial inlaid plates had once been mounted and then pried off and lost. Fortunately, the shapes of the "indents" alone were clues to whomever the stone had once memorialized. They indicated that the stone originally held three monumental metal (probably brass) plates, one in the shape of a knight in full armor, another an armorial shield, and the third a decorative scroll possibly marked with a Latin phrase (a family motto?). The excavators then logically dubbed the stone the "Knight's Tomb."

FIGURE 7.2 Belgium marble ledgerstone with a knight and armorial indents found by the APVA.

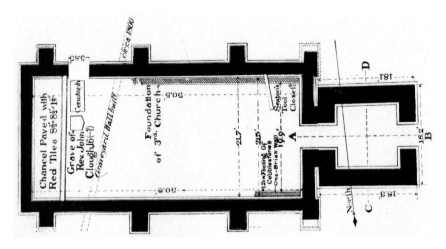

FIGURE 7.3   1902 map of APVA excavation drawn by engineer Samuel Yonge showing two periods of church foundations.

Why these stones were positioned where they were must have puzzled the excavators. Nonetheless, they "dug on" to find evidence of two or three periods of adjacent chancel tile floors and a brick chancel aisle. They concluded that the Knight's stone found in the sacred chancel must have once marked the grave of an extremely important person. They reasoned it had to have been Sir George Yeardley, the knighted Captain General and Governor of Jamestown, who died at Jamestown in 1627. The APVA excavators mapped some of what they found before filling in and leveling their excavations.

In 2017, with the 400th anniversary of the meeting of America's first democratic government on the horizon, Jamestown Rediscovery archaeologists led another excavation of the churches site with essentially the same goal as the earlier APVA's excavators. That is—to learn as much as possible about the architecture and burials of the various phases of churches, and particularly the earliest Timber Church of 1617–1639 where the first General Assembly met. This time, however, they had an additional goal: to determine if there was a burial under the Knight's tomb. After removing the stone for restoration, our excavations quickly determined that there had never been a grave under it. This meant that the Knight's tomb did not mark a tomb at all. Rather, it was re-used stone to pave the chancel aisle, moved probably during the construction of the brick church from a former position marking the original Knight's grave. In 1901, the APVA made two overall site photos of their excavation, one taken from the west from on the top of the standing ruin of the church tower and the other from the east at ground level. These photos proved critical for reaching the first step of our recent excavation: to dig inside the Memorial Church deep enough to re-expose the site as it appeared in the 1901 photos. Reaching that goal first required the removal of a wooden chancel

FIGURE 7.4   Original Jamestown church tower and the 1907 reconstruction Brick Church attached (JRF).

platform, a brick floor, and subfloor fill put in by 1907. It came as no surprise that our new excavation uncovered a tangled maze of superimposed seventeenth- to eighteenth-century archaeological features, made all the more complicated by the holes previously dug by the well-meaning APVA explorers.

Before our shovels went into the ground, though, a comprehensive systematic record search was carried out—looking for or rereading any references that might reveal details of the architectural history of the two churches. Relatively few clues were found, but one letter written by Governor Samuel Argall stated that when he arrived at Jamestown to replace Deputy Governor George Yeardley in the spring of 1617, he found a town of only "five or six houses, the Church down, the Palizados broken ... the Storehouse ... used for the Church ... [the population] ... no more than 400."[4] He then wrote that he had a "20′ by 50′ Timber Church" built. This was smaller than its predecessor, the remains of the "fallen" (24′ x 64′) building we found in 2010 forty feet to the southwest. Apparently, to Argall, the downsizing made sense because the Jamestown population was much smaller than it had been nine years earlier. By the time this church was built, most new settlers were not living at Jamestown. They had established their tobacco plantations elsewhere on the banks of the river, far from Jamestown.[5]

Besides its dimensions, there is no other known documentary description of Argall's 1617 Timber Church, other than that it had a *quire (*chancel*)* where the

FIGURE 7.5 Memorial Church interior before Jamestown Rediscovery archaeological excavations.

Source: Danny Schmidt, JRF.

governing General Assembly gathered before being seated in the "*body*" of the church and where there was a *barre* "rail" where the sergeant at arms stood ready to maintain order and security.[6] There is, however, another document which may hint indirectly about the church design. When Sir George Yeardley was about to embark for Virginia in 1618 as the newly appointed Jamestown Governor, he met with its namesake King James, who instructed him that "... o[u]r churches [in Virginia] should not be built like Theaters or Cockpitts, but in a decent forme, & in imitation of the churches in Englande."[7] Based on these instructions, it is possible to conclude that during Yeardley's first governorship he may have indeed taken the King's orders to heart, altering Argall's two-year-old structure in some way, perhaps by upgrading the chancel and/or adding a belfry. Any one or both of these changes would indeed be "in imitation" of a more typical English Church. Without that change, the Jamestown church may well indeed have looked more like a secular box ("theater") than a sanctuary. Without any surviving drawing of the structure however, archaeological research was deemed the only way to get a sense of the "body" of that early Timber Church where this first General Assembly met. It did.

FIGURE 7.6   Sections of the three churches foundations labeled 1617–1639 brick on cobble, 1640–1647 brick, and 1907 reconstruction (JRF).

Miraculously, considerable evidence of the 1617 brick-and-cobble church foundations survived, despite the disturbances made by the construction of the subsequent churches built on the site (one in the 1640s and the other in 1907) and by the APVA digging. The recent excavations uncovered parts of all four early wall footings and building details (Figure 7.6). The walls did encompass a 50′x20′ space, the overall dimensions of the church that again Argall claimed to have built.[8] In addition, our archaeologists found wall coating material with impressions of timbers indicating that the superstructure was a traditional 1/2 timber-framed building with walls plastered over mixed clay. The absence of roofing tiles in the deeper levels of destruction fill probably meant that the earlier church had a thatched roof. There was no sign of flooring material, but the deepest and therefore earliest archaeological level found consisted of original black topsoil devoid of artifacts lying beneath an accumulation of brick dust, ostensibly laid down during the construction of the 1640s brick church. This "clean" topsoil beneath the later brick dust could mean that the early church had a wooden floor built on raised sills that would leave no traces on the subfloor. Also, a single brick found bonded into the south wall at a right angle likely marked the location of a southeastern door. There was no sign of another door, but a traditional Anglican church would have had another entrance leading into

FIGURE 7.7 Section of the West Timber Church wall that lay beneath a modern concrete church tower floor.

Source: Charles Durfor, JRF.

the western end of the body of the church either toward the western end of the south wall or on the west end of the building.

Parts of the east cobble-based wall had luckily survived despite the subsequent disturbances of chancel graves over the 110-year lifespan of the Brick Church (1640–1750). Fifty feet west of that wall, more of the original west wall foundation was found inside the church tower beneath a modern concrete floor (Figure 7.7).

It was the location and survival of the section of the west wall that confirmed Argall's reported dimensions. Together, the remains of the four walls of the earlier church indicated that the 1640–1647 Brick Church had indeed been built on the razed site of its predecessor—but not exactly *right* on it (ten feet to the west).

Most of the burials the APVA excavators found were originally located beyond the east end of the Timber Church, either placed in the chancel of the Brick Church or in the ground outside the east end of the Timber Church. This 10′ offset between the two periods of churches also meant that none of "stacked" square tile chancel floors or the chancel aisle with its ledgerstone paving date from before ca. 1639. This provided more telling proof that the Knight's tomb, if it did mark Yeardley's 1627 original grave in the Timber Church, was moved from its original place somewhere in that early church and ultimately wound up as the paving stone in the 1640s Church Chancel aisle.

FIGURE 7.8   Burial found centered at the very east end of the 1617 church.
Source: Charles Durfor, JRF.

Archaeologists speculated that the "somewhere" was located where an unusually large, deep, and perfectly rectangular-shaped man's grave was found, precisely placed at the center of the very eastern end of the Timber Church. The location of this grave meant that this man was laid to rest directly under what must have been the early church altar, indicating that this was likely the grave of an especially high-ranking person like Sir George Yeardley[9] (Figure 7.8).

There is, however, substantial circumstantial evidence for another possible identification of this man. Consider that the person in the "altar" burial was purposely laid in his grave oriented east to west—that is, with his head originally at the east end.[10] That orientation was unique. The twenty other graves uncovered within the churches chancel foundations all faced west-to-east. Why the difference? According to one interpretation of "ancient Old English burial tradition," only bishops, priests, and ordained clergy could be buried with the east–west orientation, ostensibly honoring the belief that at resurrection time the cleric would rise and face his congregation.[11] It follows that lay people, even prominent individuals, would be buried in a west–east orientation with their heads to the west.

Records indicated that the Timber Church was replaced by the Brick Church by 1647, so our altar burial, located just inside the East Timber Church wall, was almost certainly buried in the church that stood from 1617 to 1640. Moreover, the east–west orientation may indicate he was a cleric. The Reverend Richard Buck died in 1623, having served 13 years as the highly respected spiritual arm of the Jamestown church. It would seem logical that Reverend Buck, the esteemed minister, would be reverently buried with his head to the east in the holiest place in the relatively new church. That prestigious place, of course, would be in the Timber Church chancel, under the altar.

There remains, however, a caveat. Buck's death left Jamestown without a minister. Perhaps the congregation was not aware of the orientation tradition and mistakenly disregarded it during George Yeardley's later burial. Given that the ledgerstone did mark this altar burial, then Yeardley himself could have been memorialized "forever" in the most sacred location in the church. In that case, however, Yeardley's Knight's stone would lay unseen under the Timber Church altar. Certainly, such an ornate memorial stone was meant to be seen. It may have been more logical to bury and memorialize Yeardley in the *quire* space in the early church, as it was there that the expensive stone would command the attention of parishioners and it was there that Yeardley had presided over the General Assembly in 1619 and 1627. Also there was enough time between Yeardley's death in November 1627 and the next Assembly meeting at the end of July 1628 to order, receive from England, and place the personalized "Knight's" ledgerstone on his grave elsewhere in the early chancel.

Our excavations had to end by 2019 so that three layers of a modern flooring could be installed and the Knight's ledgerstone placed under glass over the altar burial all in time for the first assembly commemoration. In any case, at that time, the assumption was made that this was Yeardley's grave unless proven otherwise by DNA analysis.

In 2021, America's foremost forensic anthropologist Dr. Douglas Owsley, Smithsonian National Museum of Natural History, Smithsonian's genealogist, Andrew Ramsey, and Harvard University's Dr. David Reich were able to compare the mitochondrial (female line) DNA from the early chancel burial with two living people found to be distant female line descendants of Governor Yeardley. While the modern DNA samples from the Yeardley relatives matched each other as predicted, they did not match the DNA from the chancel burial. This is now almost certain evidence that the Timber Church chancel burial was not George Yeardley. That being the case, it follows that the next logical identity for the burial could well be the aforementioned Reverend Richard Bucke.

Two other church burials then become good candidates for the Governor and likely his wife. The remains of a man and a woman were uncovered in graves located in the center of what seems to be the Brick Church "quire" (Figure 7.9). They were also found in carefully dug grave shafts deeper than and immediately east of the aisle burial. The original digging of their grave shafts could have "removed" the center section of eastern end wall of the Timber Church and, therefore, could postdate the 1617–1639 structure. In any event, nail patterns and faint signs of wood in the graves indicated that both burials had been laid to rest in identical octagonal coffins and traces of decomposed black cloth shrouded the women—possibly remnants of a black dress.[12] Forensic evidence also indicated that both individuals died when they were in their thirties.

FIGURE 7.9   A man and a women's burial found centered in the Brick Church chancel
space just east of the aisle burial. (author JRF).

Significantly, on the right side and outside of the man's coffin, the grave shaft
fill held a broken ceremonial metal staff head and its sharpened spear point foot
(Figures 7.10–7.12). These are the decorative parts of a broken Captain's Leading
Staff, a type dating from the late sixteenth to the first half of the seventeenth century. We can know the date owing to the existence of dated portraits of men holding
similar staffs, in particular the 1627–1629 portrait of Tobias Blosse, "Captain of the
trained band of the Town of Ipswich."[13] It is significant that Blosse's staff is identical to the Jamestown staff establishing that our example was indeed a captain's sign
of rank. Who, then, was this Jamestown captain? The archaeological and historical
evidence of the possible identity of the captain is complex.

There are logical two ways to explain how the Leading Staff got into the grave.
Did it arrive there by coincidence or did someone officiating at a high-ranking
captain's funeral place it there? The coincidence scenario seems possible, since the
excavation of the eastern half of his grave shaft had inadvertently dug into the fill
of a 1608–1610 pre-church building cellar. The head and foot of the broken staff
could therefore have unknowingly been dug out of the cellar fill to wind up in the
grave backfill. That is possible, since other grave fill in the north side of the chancel
held scattered displaced broken pottery that dated to that period. If, however, that is
how both the head and the foot of the broken captain's leading staff finally did wind
up in the man's grave—by coincidence—then we are still left with the question,
who was the captain whose symbol of rank has been unceremoniously discarded in
the abandoned early seventeenth-century cellar?

But what if the head and the foot of the staff were ceremoniously broken then
placed on the man's coffin or in the grave. This was an English traditional funerary

FIGURE 7.10 1627 Portrait of Captain Tobias Blosse holding his Captain's Leading Staff.

Source: Colchester Museum.

FIGURE 7.11 Close-up of staff head which is identical to the one found broken in a Jamestown church burial (Figure 7.9).

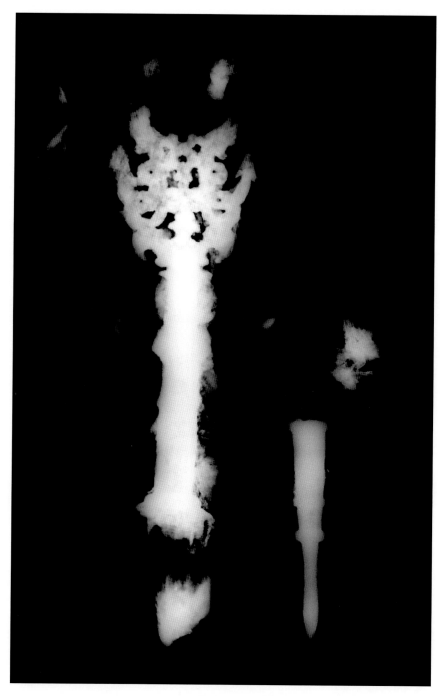

FIGURE 7.12   X ray of the broken leading staff sections found in the in the 1617–1750
Jamestown church. burial (Figure 7.9).

Source: Dan Gamble, JRF.

act to symbolize the end of a time in office. If it that is true, it would not be the first time we had found evidence of shafts in probable captain's burials at Jamestown. Possible ceremonial shafts turned up in two other graves at James Fort: one found outside the West Fort Wall, thought to be Captain Bartholomew Gosnold, and another in the 1608–1616 Church Chancel thought to be Captain Gabriel Archer.[14] From these two prior discoveries, and now the broken Captain's leading staff from the Church chancel grave, one could logically conclude that placing ceremonial staffs in high-ranking men's graves must have at least been a military tradition. We could conclude then that the third ceremonial staff found in the Church burial really was no coincidence. If true, then who was this captain, and presumably his wife, carefully laid out side by side? So could these two individuals be the Captain General and Governor Yeardley who died in 1627 around age 35 and his wife Temperance, who died at the same age?[15]

This identification is problematic. Records of the dates of their deaths do fit into the time when the Timber Church was standing, but the digging of their graves could have cut through the east Timber Church end wall. This seems to prove that they were buried in the later Brick Church. Still, their ages at death, her clothing, and their placement in the center and chancel end of the church(es) do fit with the documentary evidence for Yeardley and his wife. So we might consider this: what if Yeardley, in 1619–1620, did enlarge the chancel or add an apse to the two-year-old Timber Church in an attempt to make it more "like English Churches," as King James directed? This could mean that the two grave shafts would have cut through the center section of the "former" end wall of the Timber Church then extended on into the enlarged apse/chancel. Admittedly, little archaeological evidence of an apse/chancel addition exists, but it is also possible that the digging of the later burials in the Brick Church chancel erased all signs of it. The archaeological golden rule that "the lack of evidence is not evidence of absence" might well apply here.

But the big question remains—if there was no chancel/apse added to the Timber Church, then the man is also not Captain Yeardley. But who could he be? The answer might lie in what known Jamestown Captain is "not." For instance, the man cannot be the prominent political and military Jamestown leader Captain William Peirce, who died sometime after 1647, at about age of 67, and the woman cannot be his wife Joan Peirce, who died sometime after 1641 near the age of 61. So, while the time of death of the Pierces determined by historical records occurred when the Brick Church was standing, their ages at death do not even come close to the ages of the younger buried couple.

There are no known records of other captains buried at Jamestown after the Timber Church was replaced by the Brick Church around 1647.[16] But there are other prominent captains besides Yeardley who could have been buried in the earlier Timber Church: Captain William Powell who died in 1622 around age 42, Captain Ralph Hamor who died before 1626 at about age 36, Captain Roger Smith who died after 1629 around age 39, and Sir Captain Francis West who died in 1634 about age 42. There is no known record of their wives' names or when they died and where they were buried. Once again, it is critical to turn to mitochondrial DNA testing, comparing the DNA of chancel/apse man with the living Yeardley descendants' DNA. A match identifies him as Sir George Yeardley. A mismatch proves he is **not** Yeardley which also indicates that an **unknown** captain and his wife were buried either in an enlarged Timber Church chancel or later after 1619–1647 when the Brick Church chancel existed.[17]

In any event, the Timber Church replacement—the Brick Church—had a troubled history. First, it seems it took eight years to complete the brickwork, with a stoppage in the mid-1640s, probably when funds ran short. Then, as we know, Nathaniel Bacon's Jamestown supporter Richard Lawrence gutted the Brick Church when the town went up in flames in 1676. Apparently, one of the timber ceiling beams did fall and break the "Knight's" ledgerstone. The ruined brick shell must have been repaired sometime after 1683, when Rev. Clough's dated ledgerstone joined the Knight's stone to pave the chancel aisle. Unfortunately, no references remain describing any other details of the Brick Church except that by the early eighteenth century it had a steeple and bell(s). Its demise came when it was deconsecrated in 1758 and fell into complete ruin by the end of that century.

Again, our excavations at first "re-found" foundation sections of the Brick Church that APVA excavators had found by 1901. They were still intact beneath or inside of the 1907 Memorial Church. Overall, these foundations are about the same dimensions as the down-sized 1617 Timber Church footings, perhaps another indication that the Brick Church served a relatively small Jamestown population. We also found small sections of the two chancel tile floors that the APVA excavators had almost completely removed in order to dig into the chancel graves (Figure 7.13). On the very edge of the chancel, however, our excavations "re-discovered" some remnants of square brick tile floors and several graves that had largely escaped the APVA digging. Indications of brick floor paving in the choir and a number of disturbed and undisturbed burials lay uncovered in the Church Nave.

We also uncovered two periods or more of brick aisle paving and scattered deposits of some burned wood either laying on or beneath the layer of Brick Church construction brick dust. Significantly, all of these features rested on the original topsoil level where later building remains and burials did not cut through it. This topsoil level pre-dated the Timber and Brick churches altogether. The builders of the east foundation wall of the Brick Church also encountered the loose fill in the pre-churches 1607–1610 cellar, and realized it would not support the great weight of the east Brick Church gable wall. So they dug eight feet down until reaching a natural clay cellar floor where they could begin laying up the wall based on solid ground.

This seems to indicate that the masons had some experience with building in the clayey Virginia Tidewater region. Nonetheless, the brickwork itself appeared rather poor in all the Brick Church wall footings. Even the mortar proved to be of second rate.[18] The Brick Church sidewalls broke bond ten feet from the west wall,

FIGURE 7.13   Periods of chancel paving tiles during excavation, remnants of Bacon's fire 1676 on the second period of chancel tiles (inset).

Source: Charles Durfor, JRF.

marking a halt in construction. That probably happened in 1640, when funding had run out. The continuation of the footing indicates that after the construction hiatus a fundraising drive among the parishioners was successful enough to allow the work to carry on.

The brickwork was not carefully laid, and the lesser quality mortar seems to show that even though the project could continue it did so on a tight budget. It also appears that during the laying of the west wall foundation the masons found that the footing would run directly across a grave of someone who probably had been buried in the Timber Church. Rather than lay the wall directly on the earlier burial, the masons must have realized that if they planted the heavy wall footing directly on what might have been a freshly filled grave shaft, the heavy wall would settle into it in time. They built a crude arch over the loose grave fill to solve the problem. This perhaps represents another indication of the mason's level of experience.

It seems the tight Brick Church building budget did not rule out some measure of architectural fenestration. Footings were found extending at a right angle from and flanking the center of the west wall, which must have functioned as underlying supports for a brick entrance portico, apparently of classical design. A section of a brick pedestal and a brick abraded into a half column were found in destruction debris near the church, likely discarded parts of a crude classical column portico. It apparently served as the original entrance to the Brick Church and was then later bonded into the church tower.

The exact construction date of the tower remains unknown, but it would be a logical addition to the restored Brick Church after the 1676 Bacon's Rebellion fire.

FIGURE 7.14   Break in the east face of the church tower apparently showing signs where a bonded brick portico had fallen away around the doorway.

Source: APVA.

It was, however, not quite an "addition." The tower curiously stood nine inches from the Brick Church west end wall. Why the gap? One explanation could be that the tower masons retained some of the Brick Church portico walls and roof in some way and bonded them into the tower wall.[19] This makes some sense. If the portico connected to both the Brick Church wall and the tower, its roof could protect the church entrance doorway from rain trickling down the nine-inch gap. When the ruins of the body of the Brick Church collapsed, the attached portico surround fell away, leaving what appears to be a porch-shaped hole on each side of the tower's east ground floor doorway. The tower-church gap also gave the masons room enough to lay in mortar joints in that space, course by course, as the tower wall went up. Still, that tower wall surface in the very narrow gap was almost inaccessible to the masons. They therefore laid only roughly aligned brick courses while the three other tower walls, built out in the open, could be more easily made straight and true.

From structural details, it becomes clear that the Brick Church builders wisely understood the downward as well as the outward pressure of the brick walls. Again, they took pains to find a firm clay base to support the heavy walls. They also almost certainly took into account the outward force of a heavy roof by installing eight brick support columns as buttresses: two at the west corners, four spaced along the north and south walls, and two almost but not quite opposite the northeast and southeast corners. The buttresses were not afterthoughts—their foundations were bonded to the main Brick Church walls, indicating that they were not additions to shore up the existing walls during the post-Bacon's Rebellion fire renovations.

Many architectural scholars believed that the overall design of the Jamestown Brick Church came from the seventeenth-century St. Luke's Church, Smithfield, which still stands. More recent research has refuted that claim. Dendrochronology (tree ring patterns) of an original St. Lukes timber dated it to the 1670s.[20] It follows

FIGURE 7.15   St. Luke's "Gothic-esque" Church, Smithfield Virginia showing brick buttresses not unlike the buttresses that once shored up the Jamestown church walls (see Figure 7.4).

Source: Virginia Tourism Corporation.

then that the buttresses on the 1639–1647 Jamestown Brick Church seem to be the earliest example of Gothic-like architectural elements of American churches.

The existence and position of the Jamestown church buttresses seem to be clues to the engineering design of the superstructure. If so, the northwest and southwest corner buttresses make sense, since the weight of the gable end probably did require the heavy support at those corners. That being the case, it remains puzzling why the buttresses at the east end of the building were built three feet short of directly opposing the east gable wall and ostensibly not built there to strengthen it. By the time more funds came through in the 1640s, the construction delay may have brought on a whole new crew of masons who for some reason did not know that the buttresses were not just decorative.

In any case, our archaeology discoveries at the churches' site once again enabled us to reach back in time through analyses of its design details and in some ways touched the workmen who created it. In the future, we hopefully can connect with some of the Brick Church period parishioners by recovering and "reconstructing" biographies through the forensic analysis of their skeletal remains. Here again, like the Statehouse complex, our church study serves as a telling example that Bacon's attempt to uproot icons of the Jamestown "establishment" for good proved a complete failure. For the next 70 years, the renovated Brick Church continued to dominate the Jamestown landscape, a powerful architectural symbol of the favored upper-class elites.

Notes

1 The archaeological and documentary history of the churches is explained in detail in David Givens, Mary Anna Hartley, Dr. James Horn, and Michael Lavin, *Church and State: The Archaeology of the Foundations of Democracy, 1619–2019* (Williamsburg, VA: The Jamestown Rediscovery Foundation and Preservation, 2020). Some of that narrative is summarized in this chapter along with my discussion of more of the story that I feel stems from my own research and my own interpretation of the evidence.

2 Clough could have died eight years earlier after he was captured by Bacon and condemned to death. But he was pardoned probably because he was a cleric.

3 Op. cit. Neville, Bacon's Rebellion, 312.

4 Op. cit. Haile, Jamestown Narratives. 907.

5 Op. cit. Barbour, Smith 11 262, Samuel Argall and John Rolfe signed the letter.

6 John Pory. "An Account of the Proceedings of the First General Assembly, July 30th – August 4th, 1619", the National Archives, Kew, CO 1/1.

7 The Letters of John Chamberlain (The Philadelphia Philosophical Society, 1939), II 188.

8 Again, these archaeological discoveries are described in great detail in Givens et al. Church and State, passim.

9 As it turned out, trying to prove beyond reasonable doubt who he is would take a major scientific, forensic, and genealogical effort that, at this writing, was still in progress.

10 The missing skull had been removed by the disturbance of a later grave but it was recovered by excavations a few feet to the southeast.

11 Notes on Ceremonial from the Ancient English Office Books, Directions for…Funerals, Pickering and Chatto (London, 1888), 172. Even the unceremonious grave of King

Richard III, recently found buried at Leicester UK, held to tradition with his head to the west.

12 Dr. Douglas Owsley, Head of Physical Anthropology, the National Museum of Natural History, Smithsonian Institution. Personal communication.

13 I am most grateful to Barry Tsirelson and Andrew Ramsey for identifying this portrait.

14 Kelso, *Jamestown The Buried Truth*, 142; Kelso, *Jamestown, The Truth Revealed*, 174. The possible Gosnold staff appeared not to be broken but it was probably a spear instead of a Captain's Leading staff.

15 Owsley, personal communication.

16 However, future genealogical record searches may find candidates.

17 Other Captains in the Fort for whom we do not have their ages at death are Captain Percy captain of fifty, Captain George Webb sergeant major of the Fort, Captain Edward Bruster "who hath command of His Honor's own company," Captain Thomas Lawson, Captain Thomas Holecroft, Master Ralph Hamor probable captains: Master Browne, clerks of the council and Master Daniel Tucker and Master Robert Wilde. There are no known captains who died after 1647.

18 Givens et al., *Church and State*, 26.

19 Carl Lounsbury, personal communication.

20 Worthington, M. J., and Miles, *The Tree-Ring Dating of Timbers from St. Luke's Church (also known as Newport Parish Church or Old Brick Church* (Smithfield, Isle of Wight County, Virginia, 2008), unpublished report.

8

VANISHING ISLAND

Dr. John Cotter, a pioneer in the field of historical archaeology, directed excavations of the Jamestown National Park Service property from 1955 to 1957. He opened up literally miles of trenches in a 100-foot grid system. He also carried out very limited tests on the adjacent Association for the Preservation of Virginia Antiquities (APVA) property, in a search for any traces of the 1607 James Fort. He did not find any trace of the fort and agreed with conventional wisdom that it had washed away. He rushed excavation in order to ready the town site for a projected pilgrimage of visitors gathering for the 350th anniversary of the founding of Jamestown in 1957. Soon afterward, Cotter finished his digging and produced a monumental account of his excavations, as well as all other previous Jamestown excavations that he could document, beginning with the APVA reports of their work inside the memorial church from 1890 to 1902. After chronicling all of his archaeological efforts, he wrote: "in 1957 systematic trench testing at Jamestown ended, it is hoped forever. New field techniques employing ... such devices as a proton magnetometer which employs nuclear resonance to detect underground features without excavating should be employed at Jamestown." When he wrote this, his thinking was probably influenced by the fact that he had become completely exhausted, having dug trenches through what he estimated was 10 acres of the 20-acre main town site in only 18 months. He once told me that he knew that this was too much dirt moving to adequately record and fully understand what was found. After the dust settled, he concluded that, since archaeology is basically a destructive process, he could predict a high tech, non-digging future. He felt the archaeological story of Jamestown could eventually be discovered without lifting a shovel. He was partially right.[1]

Today, there are indeed more modern ways to seek archaeological evidence beyond Cotter's magnetometer. In the 60 years since his time, tools, such as

DOI: 10.4324/9781003441670-8

ground-penetrating radar (GPR), a process that sends rebounding radar waves into the ground to digitally see buried features, produce a map of "anomalies" to guide digging. To a greater or lesser degree of confidence, the digital images can become excavation "targets." The targets then require digging to identify them, a process that has become known as "ground truthing." Until recently, in my experience, the targets have often turned out to be false signals of anything from rotten tree roots to modern lightening rod cables.

The new and improved GPR instruments can, however, sometimes miraculously pinpoint buried archaeological remains. One GPR test of a space once trenched tested by Cotter, for example, produced a digital map precisely depicting a four-bastion classic star-shaped fort[2] (Figure 8.1 and 8.2). This was known as the "Turf Fort" in the seventeenth century, and represents an extraordinarily significant you-are-here find. A 1665 Jamestown land patent describes "ye Eastern Bastions of an old Ruin'd Turf Fort" as the eastern boundary line of a certain property. Finding the location of that patent today required knowing where exactly the fort and bastions had stood, but no sign of this fort remained on the ground. Now, however, the GPR discovery clearly shows the Turf Fort bastion datum points from which that

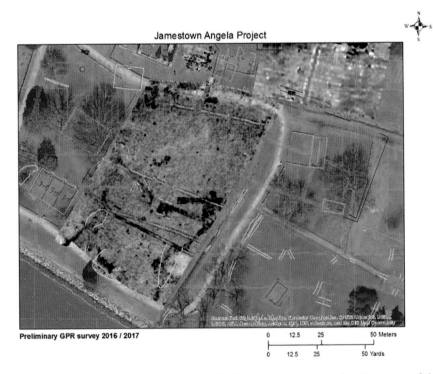

FIGURE 8.1 A gound-penetrating radar (GPR) screen image showing the traces of the ditches of a star-shaped fort.

Source: Davird Givens, Pete Leach, JRF, GSSI.

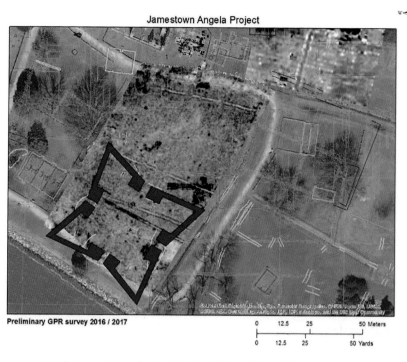

Preliminary GPR survey 2016 / 2017

FIGURE 8.2   Interpreted readout of the buried star-shaped Jamestown Turf Fort marked in in blue.

Source: David Givens, Peter Leach, JRF GSSI.

one property and indeed other connecting adjacent seventeenth-century Jamestown properties patents can—at long last—be located on the ground without "putting a shovel in the ground."[3]

How can a leveled earthen fort produce a GPR signature? It likely sensed filled-in ditches that made up the fort moats. These earthen forts were first built by digging a conjoined star-shaped ditch that would become the fort moat, all the while piling the excavated dirt on one side of the moat to create an equally star-shaped earthen wall. Then, when the fort became obsolete, these mounds became a hindrance to plowing as the site of Jamestown was transformed into agricultural fields. Apparently, at that time, the earthen walls were pushed back into the moat to level the site for plowing. The fort visibly disappeared. Nonetheless, the leveled fort showed on the GPR readout because it sensed the less compact soil in the filled moated outer star. The radar signal would go deep into the moat fill to rebound off the harder natural clay bottom of the former moat ditch. Now, without a doubt, ground truthing excavations across the ditches shown on the GPR map can reveal the enclosure and uncover the actual total fort plan.

Cotter's insinuation, however, that "hi tech" archaeology would protect the island's rich buried history from archaeologist's potentially destructive shovels is only partially good advice. Another force has impacted the archaeological sites on the low-lying island even more: erosion. It has really been nature, and not man, that has proven to eat away Jamestown's archaeological sites dating back to the very beginning of the colony. The cartographic and photographic history of Jamestown Island proves it.

Who could blame Dr. Philip Barbour, the foremost twentieth-century Jamestown historian when he wrote that "archaeological evidence can prove nothing, for the undoubted site has been washed into the James River."[4]

All references to the forts' location supported that conclusion. For instance, George Percy emphatically stated in 1607 that Jamestown Island was chosen for the site of James Fort because the river channel was close enough to the shore to moor the ships to the trees. Today, and for centuries, the closest the channel comes to the fort site is about a half mile—far beyond the reach of any mooring lines. Based on that fact alone, almost everyone concluded that the fort had been built on the ground on the extreme west end of the island, ground that had indeed totally washed away. No document, however, ever actually stated that the fort was built at that first landing point. Still, for at least 250 years, the misreading of the land and period maps also supported the lost-to-erosion story, until, as we now know, most of the fort site was discovered hiding in plain site on high dry ground.

Why did so many people conclude that the fort site was dissolved on the western end of the island? During my research, prior to beginning our excavations in April 1994, period map comparison actually seemed to prove the pessimistic western-end erosion theory. For example, in 1686, John Soane, a surveyor, drew a plat of Jamestown for resident William Sherwood showing Sherwood's recently acquired land on the island (Figure 8.3). In doing so, he drew landscape features along the west end of the island, including a 2000-foot stretch of James River shoreline from the "isthmus"—the low tide connection of Jamestown Island to the mainland—to just beyond a small creek-like arm of a marsh the colonists had named the "Pitch and Tar" swamp. He also located a "blockhouse hill" near the isthmus, as well as a Shoreline Road from the isthmus to a point beyond the Pitch and Tar swamp. Significantly, this map shows in great detail the configuration of the island's western shoreline as it was in 1686. Consequently, the map established a baseline for comparison with later shoreline maps, offering us a chance to define precisely how much land was lost over time.

A comparison with a map drawn about 100 years after Soane's defines the extent of missing land.[5] During the American Revolution, when the French army arrived in Virginia prior to joining the Americans at the Battle of Yorktown in 1781, a French engineer named Nicholas Desandrouin made detailed maps of the lower peninsula—especially the Williamsburg area—from the York River to the James River shores (Figure 8.4). His maps have proven amazingly accurate, particularly their location of buildings and other details of the terrain including roads, fences, and wooded areas. One of Desandrouin's maps showed Jamestown Island.

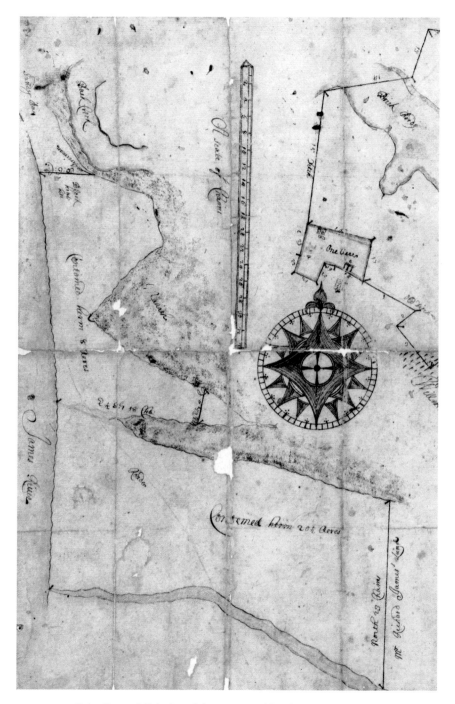

FIGURE 8.3   John Soane 1681 plat of the western side of Jamestown Island.

Source: Colonial Williamsburg Foundation.

FIGURE 8.4 Nicholas Desandrouin map 1781 showing the west end of Jamestown Island, and the location of a blockhouse (top) and the powder magazine. (bottom).

Source: Library of Congress.

Assuming that it is as trustworthy as it has proven for other building locations in the Williamsburg area, then the location of the Jamestown buildings and position of the shoreline must be accurate. Some of these Jamestown features also appear on the previously mentioned Soane map, which establishes points of reference for making an overlay comparison of the two.

Both maps show what appear to be the blockhouse location and the course of the mainland road along the island's western shoreline. The Soane map merely shows "blockhouse hill," but no blockhouse. Nonetheless, clearly "blockhouse hill" must have once been the location of a blockhouse, undoubtedly the one mentioned by John Smith as early as 1609, and the hill must have always been the logical location of replacement blockhouses.

The Desandrouin map shows a building on what appears to be the hill location. It is not identified as a blockhouse, but there is every reason to assume that it is. So, despite the fact that 100 years had elapsed between the production of the Soane and Desandrouin maps, the blockhouse site appears to have survived erosion. That defendable location always made sense. The construction of a blockhouse where the isthmus met the west end of the island created a strategic "gate" to protect the island from invaders—first Virginia Indians, then the Dutch in the 1660s, Nathaniel Bacon's rebels in 1776, and finally the British in 1781. Fortunately, the blockhouse site serves as a common comparison point to define how much shore erosion occurred over almost a century, from 1686 to 1781.

Desandrouin's map also shows a building symbol about 100 yards from the southwestern shoreline. This building must be the 1690s powder magazine that was standing when the artist John Sully drew it at some distance from a seriously eroded Jamestown shore in 1854.[6] Another drawing attributed to Sully, however,

FIGURE 8.5   Jamestown Powder Magazine before shoreline erosion destroyed it.

Source: Julia Sulley Papers, Smithsonian Institution.

FIGURE 8.6   Remains of the powder magazine vaulted cellar as it eroded into the river
With the "Shoreline Road" to the "lone" cypress and the river channel in
the background (1880s?).

Source: Courtsey of Anthony Opperman.

shows the magazine as a ruin in the same year. Another undated drawing apparently shows what remained of the magazine as it was tumbling into the river around
1870, as well as what seems to show a road connecting the shore to a wharf and
cypress tree at the river channel.

Another feature common to both the 1683 Soane and the 1781 Desandrouin
map, the Shoreline Road, makes possible a more precise comparison of the two
documents. No reason exists to think that the road changed course over time.
A comparison of the land shown between the road and the shoreline clearly

FIGURE 8.7   The historian traveler Benson Lossing's sketch of Jamestown Island in
1851 (church tower and Church Point center background).

FIGURE 8.8   The probable "carriage road" to the lone cypress tree in background shown on an undated photograph probably taken in the 1880s.

Source: APVA.

FIGURE 8.9   Painting of the western shoreline of Jamestown Island probable vestiges of "the old Church Point" in the background.

Source: APVA.

indicates that much of the west end of the island, and more land toward the south, was lost during the intervening century. The scale of the maps suggests that this land loss amounted to at least 150 feet of shoreline at the isthmus to 340 feet opposite the Pitch and Tar swamp. It follows that had the 1607 fort actually been located directly on this western shore, then its archaeological remains would have been destroyed as early as 1781. The Soane map was not available for pre-excavation research in 1993, which proved a very good thing. The actual documented shoreline loss, not just the supposition of shoreline loss, would have made a strong argument against even attempting to find any archaeological evidence of the 1607 fort at all.

There is documentary and imagery evidence, though, that the Shoreline Road existed until at least the late nineteenth century. In 1851, traveling historian Benson Lossing visited Jamestown Island and wrote:

Already a large portion of it [the island], whereon the ancient town was erected, has been washed away; and I was informed that a cypress-tree, now many yards from the shore stood at the end of a carriage-way to the wharf, sixty yards from the water's edge, only sixteen years ago. The destructive flood is gradually approaching the old church tower, and if the hand of man shall not arrest its sure progress, that too will be swept away, and not a vestige of Jamestown will remain. ... Some remains of the old fort may be seen at low water, several yards from the shore.[7]

Another map more precisely shows the erosion of Church Point (Figure 8.10). That map charts the James River depths along the Jamestown Island south shore, showing channel soundings as well as prominent Jamestown Island shoreline features, such as split rail fences, cultivated fields, marsh-like symbols, the church tower, and the eighteenth-century Ambler family plantation mansion.

The church tower and the mansion survive today, and can serve as a way to compare the 1856 shoreline with a modern aerial photograph. In the intervening 150 years, this overlay indicated that the western end of the island lost much more land since 1781, from 75 to 300 feet of shoreline, including the "Church Point." There can be no doubt that erosion had gradually become the major force erasing archaeological sites like the powder magazine and much of the south-end building of the Statehouse Complex (see Chapter 4).

Another map was drawn in 1893 when the owner of the island, E.E. Barney, deeded 22 1/2 acres to the APVA[8] (Figure 8.11). It marks more precisely the estimated shoreline of 1873–1875 compared with the existing line in 1892, showing that 180 more feet of land was eroded away on the west end of the island. It showed a diminishing loss of land to the east, however, and no erosion just east of the church.

Finally, a map of the island made in 1905, in comparison with both the Desandrouin and 1856 maps and early photographs, proves that even yet another sizable portion of the west end had melted away by the dawn of the twentieth century[9] (Figure 8.12). By that time, there was only a "lone Cypees" tree left standing

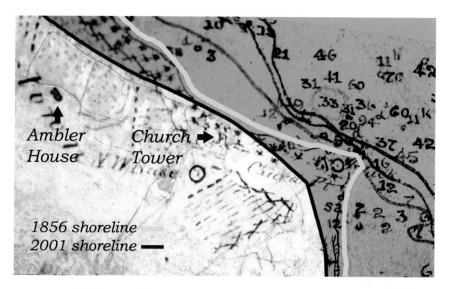

Ambler
House

Church →
Tower

1856 shoreline
2001 shoreline ▬

FIGURE 8.10   1856 map of the western end of Jamestown Island showing that Church
Point (yellow edge line) once reached out to the deep river channel but it
had eroded completely away by 2003 (red line) (National Oceanigraphic
and Atmospheric Administration). Note the church tower and the seventeenth-century Amber Plantation ruins (red arrows) are the datum points
for this overlay (National Oceanigraphic and Atmospheric Administration).

Source: Jamie May, JRF.

250 feet off the shore to mark the lost Shoreline Road. This tree also took on the
myth that it not only marked the lost Shoreline Road but also the "lost" 1607 fort.
Prophetically, the tree stood until a storm blew it over in 1994, the very year we
began to discover signs that 90 percent of the fort site survived 1000 feet to the
east, thanks to the APVA's solid stone seawall that ended its erosion in 1901–1906.

In fact, before any of our digging, one map convinced me that the fort site did not
wind up in the river.[10] In the early years of the twentieth century, the engineer Colonel Samuel Yonge, who excavated at the aforementioned statehouse site, became
familiar with the hydrographic situation of Jamestown Island when he was in charge
of constructing the seawall. Yonge studied river erosion patterns, the river channel,
and land plats showing the western island shore. He first calculated that the water
abrasion did not occur on the island until about 1700. At that time, Yonge reasoned,
a shoreline headland just upriver from Jamestown eroded to the point that it could
no longer block the brunt of wind-driven waves headed for the island. He believed
that after that protective upriver landform disappeared the island shoreline erosion
accelerated, especially on the western shore where the prevailing northwest winds
had miles of open water to create serious destructive wave action. He calculated that
this force eroded about two feet of shoreline a year until 1860. He calculated that,

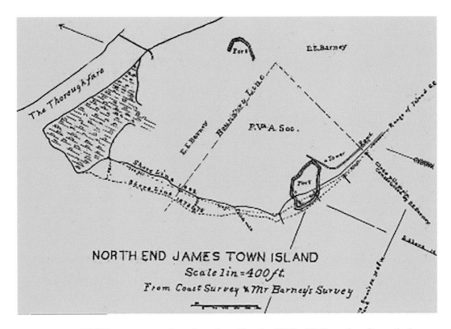

NORTH END JAMES TOWN ISLAND
Scale 1in=400ft.
From Coast Survey & Mr Barney's Survey

FIGURE 8.11   E.E. Barney map showing shoreline in 1873–1875 and as it eroded away
by 1893.

Source: Association for the Preservation of Virginia Antiquities.

after that date, an additional two feet of shoreline per year disappeared owing to a
new threat: waves created by side-wheeler steamships. Based on all of these factors,
he figured that the western shoreline had receded 482 feet between 1607 and 1901.

Yonge also concluded that, despite the violent erosion history of the island's
western shore, erosion did not completely erase the James Fort site. He felt the fort
was located farther to the east. He mapped the river channel and found that it would
have almost touched the island at a then-vanished point of land jutting out into the
river, the aforementioned Church Point. He thought that this had to be the only landing point where the settlers could "tie their ships to the shore" and easily unload their
provisions, especially their heavy ordnance. There was higher ground just east of
Church Point, however. Yonge concluded that the settlers chose this higher ground
to build the fort and actually drew an outline of the part of the triangular fort he
thought survived. He proved brilliantly close, only about a 100 feet off, but he wrote
that the fort site had probably eroded away after all. That discrepancy was puzzling,
but Yonge's map was enough to convince me in the beginning of our archaeological
project that some fragment of James Fort likely did lay in the church tower yard and
under the adjacent Confederate earthwork. I would think Yonge would be pleased to
know that it did and that his concrete seawall had essentially saved it all.

It is true that Yonge's wall saved most of the fort site—so far, but the threat of
ultimately losing the fort to erosion remains. By 2006, groundwater and possibly

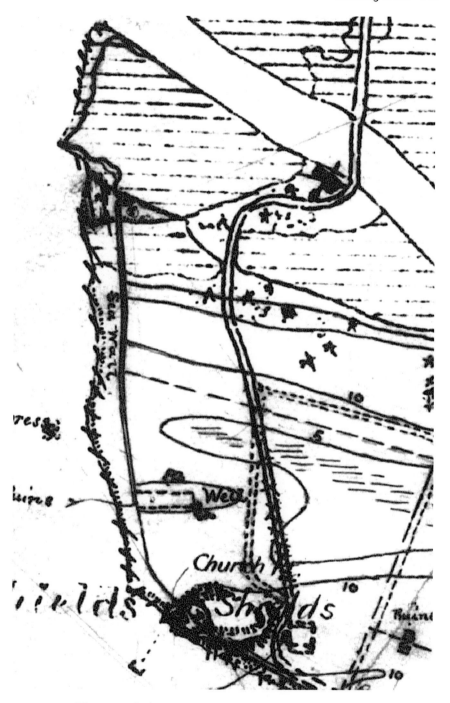

FIGURE 8.12 Western end of Jamestown Island 1905, note a lone cypress tree and the Church Point road eroded away (JRF).

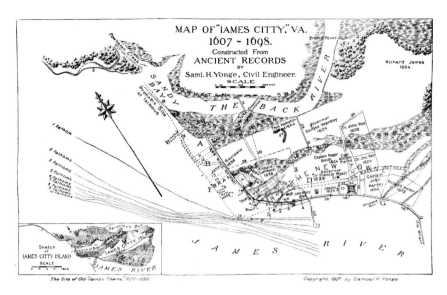

FIGURE 8.13   1901 Samuel Yonge map showing where he thought the fort had been located (small number 46) but his text announced he actually thought that the fort land had been washed away (JRF).

FIGURE 8.14   Erosion of the Civil War earthwork (mounds), the church tower, and the cliff exposing in profile the remains of James Fort shortly before Col. Samuel Yonge directed the construction of the seawall in 1901. He may have thought that the wall might turn out to save the archaeological remains of James Fort.

Source: Author's collection.

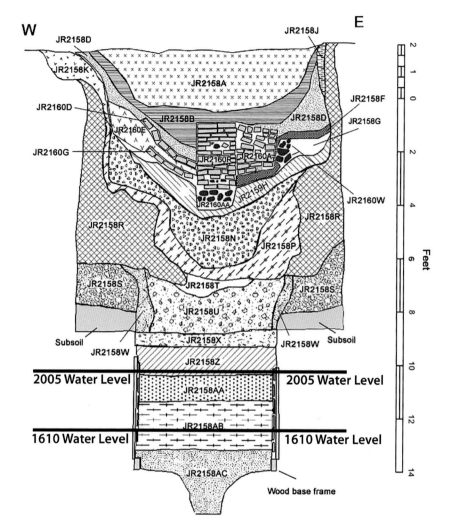

W · E

JR2158D · JR2158J
JR2158K · JR2158A
JR2158F
JR2160D · JR2158B · JR2158D · JR2158G
JR2160F
JR2160G · JR2160R · JR2160A
JR2159H
JR2160AA · JR2160W
JR2158R · JR2158R
JR2158N · JR2158P
JR2158S · JR2158T · JR2158S
JR2158U
Subsoil · JR2158X · JR2158W · Subsoil
JR2158W
JR2158Z
2005 Water Level · **2005 Water Level**
JR2158AA
JR2158AB
1610 Water Level · **1610 Water Level**
JR2158AC
Wood base frame

Feet

FIGURE 8.15 Cross-section drawing of timber-lined well made after archaeological excavation in 2005, showing ground water level in 2005 and the level when it was built in 1610, a two-foot rise in four centuries.[12]

the sea level had risen two feet.[11] We can know this because the 1610 water level in a well we dug in 2006 almost certainly never dropped. We knew that because in 1610 the well water level created an anaerobic (low oxygen) environment that completely preserved the bottom two feet of the timber well lining. We also found that the water level in 2006 was two feet above the top of the preserved wood, apparently proving that the water table had risen two feet since 1610.

Today, current hydrographic research shows that the sea level at Jamestown could rise over six feet by the end of this century[13] (Figure 8.16). That prediction

FIGURE 8.16   Sea level in 2005 (blue left), and projected level in 2100 (right), at the site of James Fort and Jamestown (green).

Source: National Oceanographic Atmospheric Administration.

has the fort and statehouse sites each becoming small islands by 2100, and most of the surrounding Jamestown Island essentially gone. This sounds quite an alarm bell, since an archaeological survey of the entire island shoreline located dozens of sites in 2010. Many of them have already begun eroding away and others will soon disappear. A comprehensive archaeological rescue effort is desperately needed, and/or major shoreline protection. Those mitigation measures are now slowly being implemented. Whether or not environmental conditions can be changed to slow or even reverse this destructive rising tide remains to be seen.

Notes

1 Op. cit. Cotter. Archeological Excavations 166.
2 Ground Penetrating Radar Test, 2015.
3 Will Riley, New Town Property Report. Mss, Jamestown Rediscovery Foundation.
4 Op. cit. Barbour I, 234, fn 9.
5 Nicolas Desandrouin, Rochambeau Collection #57, Library of Congress.
6 John Sully (1854), collection of Julia Sulley, Richmond, VA.
7 Benson J. Lossing, *The Pictorial Field-Book of the Revolution, II* (New York: Harper & Bros., 1851–52), Chapter 9.
8 E.E. Barney, Association for the Preservation of Virginia Antiquities, APVA collections.
9 1905 Engineers Map, APVA collections.
10 Op. cit. Yonge, Old Jamestown, "Map of James Citty, VA", np.
11 Kelso, Jamestown, *The Truth Revealed*, 228.
12 William Kelso, and Beverly Straube, Jamestown Rediscovery team. 2000–2006 Interim Report, 71.
13 Goodall J. Virginia, *The Impact of Climate Change on Virginia Coastal Areas* (Washington, DC, Academy of Science, 2005). National Oceanic and Atmospheric Administration, Regional Scenarios, 6.

EPILOGUE

Since the publication of my first two books the *Buried Truth* and *The Truth Revealed,* I have heard people telling me time and time again: "you have rewritten the Jamestown story." I am not naïve enough to agree. Long before we put a shovel in the ground, the basic Jamestown American "creation" story had been told and retold based on historical accounts alone. So far, the major archaeological material discoveries have primarily been interpreted in light of those "words," but I would be the last person to diminish in the slightest the enormous contribution to Jamestown history that first 25 years of archaeological research has achieved. What are those contributions to date?

Overall, adding a powerful third dimension and sense of realism to what we thought we already knew about Jamestown certainly represents no small accomplishment. Unearthing an object last touched four centuries ago, by characters known only from their written words, in a very real sense transforms who they were and what they did. That process comes as close as one can get to time travel. Bare facts have come to life, an empathetic process revealing daily life at James Fort for the English and, surprisingly, for the Powhatan.

Beyond lending a powerful sense of past reality, however, the archaeological discoveries revealed in those first two Jamestown archaeology books and this one add remarkable new perspectives to those traditional Jamestown narratives, especially those that characterized most of the original settlers as nothing more than "lazy" gentlemen. Some of them had to design and build the fort and its buildings. Others were specialists who carried out scientific experiments searching for ways to capitalize on the natural resources of Virginia. Again, it has also now become clear to me that the Indians were on both sides of the palisade, as evidenced by the things made in the traditional Indian fashion in the fort. The discovery of cannibalized remains graphically shows how close Jamestown came to becoming a second "Lost Colony" during a "Starving Time" in 1609–1610. Yet it carried on. The size and location of the first substantive church emphasize that religion functioned not just as a side issue for the Virginia Company, as some scholars suggest, and surprisingly that some colonists in the Jamestown Reformation church held Catholic beliefs. Many of the fine artifacts found left in the fort testify that early life on the far-flung reaches of the Virginia frontier did not seem to affect the status ladder.

The *Buried Truth* ended with the suggestion that the American dream was born at Jamestown in 1607. Based on the archaeological discoveries chronicled in *The Truth Revealed*, however, it seems more accurate to say that English America was all but stillborn; the growing pains excruciating; the Company town atmosphere stifling; and that the American dream a nightmare for the Virginia Indians. Nonetheless, the Virginia experimental years taught the English that the chance for a successful life in America could only come if they could get a piece of the action—the land itself. It was really at that point that the American dream began.

Now, *Remains to be Seen* tells more of the Jamestown archaeological story across two centuries. We can now know more about the material development of Jamestown, i.e., the evolution of James Fort into a more solid military design, the buried fabric of Jamestown as a major port of oceanic trade, the fiery destruction of the town during Bacon's Rebellion, the possible site of the earliest slave quarter in Virginia, the architectural development, and the burial practices in the final two Jamestown/James City churches. But the loss of island land—and consequently Jamestown archaeological sites—by rising sea level past and future has been and will continue to erase history unless serious rescue excavations and engineering mitigation measures are taken. Fortunately, the search for more buried truth so far continues. What that future research will add to a better understanding the Jamestown story "remains to be seen."

APPENDIX

HISTORICAL ARCHAEOLOGY

"How do you know that," the skeptics of our Jamestown archaeological discoveries understandably ask. The quick answer is "we use a process known as Historical Archaeology blending fact and artifact in our quest to materialize the Jamestown past." The next question is obvious, what exactly is this "historical archaeology"? Here is my answer.

First, we need a definition of the process. The name sounds like digging at sites for which there is a written history, like the archaeological study of the ancient Greeks and Romans. But while the archaeology of those ancient times and places are technically exercises in historical archaeology, the field that has become known as Historical Archaeology means, archaeological studies of literate societies from the time of the early European voyages of discovery to the present day. So historical archaeology is very time specific. It is also space specific. Primarily, it is the archaeological and historical study of sites in the "New World." But what is this "New World"? Simply put it is whatever part of the earth *not* considered the "Old World." So by definition, the New World is not made up exclusively of Columbus "discoveries" of the West Indies and the "discoveries" of North, Central, and South America that followed but it could and does as easily include, say, Australia.

Another important part of defining the historical archaeology process is that "discovery" is its primary goal. What does discovery mean? To the adventurers in the "age of discovery," it meant: finding and learning about things in the New World to contribute to the knowledge of those in the Old World. At that time, discovery did not mean what it commonly does today: finding something no other human being had ever found before. Rather, the root meaning of the word "discovery" is simply defined as the act of discovering something that was unknown to enlighten the unknowing. In this sense, Columbus really did "discover" America. He "investigated" the land and its people to enlighten his unknowing Spanish sponsors. By the same token, 115 years later Captain John Smith discovered Virginia. He surveyed and mapped the Chesapeake region for his reports to enlighten his unknowing sponsor, the Virginia Company. We can also say that Pocahontas actually discovered England when she arrived there with her Virginia Indian companion, Tomocomo in 1616. In fact, Tomocomo had a specific discovery assignment: to tally the total population of England by notching a stick for every person he saw. The marked stick was to be his "discovery" report for his fellow Virginia Indians so that they could understand how strong in numbers the English invaders actually were. Needless to say, Tomocomo soon learned how impossible his discovery mission turned out to be. But the point is, Columbus, John Smith, Pocahontas, and Tomocomo were true discoverers. So are historical archaeologists; they discover the recent past, primarily in the New World.

My own particular "New World" for the purposes of this book is the *Historical Archaeology* of Jamestown, during the time when it was a remote English foothold in the "new" land of Virginia (1607) until the end of the seventeenth century. That is not to say that I am blind to the archaeology of America that lies beyond seventeenth-century British Colonial Virginia nor European worldwide migration *per se* or to the pre-discovery period of New World peoples. Those stories are largely outside of my own experience and therefore whatever is unique to that study I leave to others more versed in that time period, those places, and other cultures.

It should also be stated upfront that underlying all my own "practice" in historical archaeology (and I am convinced that it is indeed something one "does") assumes a number of things. First and foremost is the assumption that there is indeed something that is true and knowable about the past and that by following the research process of historical archaeology one is capable of discovering something that is indeed knowledge of the past. But what is the nature of this "knowledge."

First of all, the process has its limits. I am painfully aware that should the research process of historical archaeology lead to knowledge that *appears* to be true about the past that does not mean it really *is* true. I think at best historical archaeologists can only try to find out what is *probably* true about the past. Why? It seems obvious to me that we can never be sure we know the past primarily because it *is* past. After all, seventeenth-century Jamestown is older than any live eye-witness who could tell us firsthand something about that place and time that we might want to know. And unfortunately, it is impossible to physically revisit the past in a time machine to seek some firsthand knowledge of it. Yet even if it were possible to revisit a past Jamestown, it is vital to understand that we would shape whatever we witness by experiencing it through the veil of our own time and place. So does that mean we are stuck with the inevitability that we can only understand what has passed in light of our personal life experiences? Fortunately, the answer is probably no. An effort to at least try to recognize how 400 years can cloud our lenses must be made. So even given these seemingly insurmountable stumbling blocks, we may still be left with the belief, as I am, that historical archaeology has a "chance" of leading to the acquisition of true knowledge about Jamestown of the distant past.

Of course, the process may also lead us to *false* knowledge, which is not very useful. How to recognize and avoid that, I admit, is a challenge. Could this challenge be met by applying the most rigorous rules of logic to whatever evidence *seems* impartial and to whatever conclusion (knowledge) it *seems* to produce? In fact, in reality that exercise involves examining an interrelation and sequence of known facts or events that *appear* to establish a conclusion that becomes inevitable (true knowledge). For example, if we discover that a past fact A is the same as a past fact B and a past fact B is the same as a past fact C, then it logically follows that fact A was the same as fact C, in the past. But this all assumes that A, B, and C were actually the same in the past as they are today. That is hard to know. After all, our exemplar A B Cs "are" indeed in the past and the past is beyond the backward reach of the present. So it follows that we need more than pure logic to reach the goal of true knowledge. In fact, I think our logical conclusion must draw on a certain measure of something else. I would call that *imagination*, that is "the act of forming a mental image of something incompletely present to the senses nor perceived in reality." So such is the nature of the past, certainly incompletely present to the senses and *somewhat* imperceptible in present reality.

But the past that is "incompletely present to the senses" can be logically imagined—cautiously. Historical archaeologists do not make things up. Rather, that ever-present vacuum between past and present may be to a certain degree filled with "informed" imagination; some refer to it as "a leap of faith." So with a logical base that includes our own imagination, it seems that the process of historical archaeology can at least come up with a conclusion that is, well, *likely* to be true.

So how can we be sure that our conclusion or *knowledge* is, in fact, likely true knowledge? This again highlights the fact that we have that pesky problem with certainty, a dilemma. But there is hope. The trick is to attempt to separate the *probable* from the *possible*. That difference is critical. Almost anything is possible. So accepting a certain possibility about the past really gets us nowhere in our quest for true knowledge. On the other hand, to determine probabilities, that is to say the *likelihood* that so and so is true, seems to be an improvement. But then the question remains how to cross the *possible-to-probable red* line.

It might *seem* that there is a simple solution to crossing that line. Some might say that one goes from the possible to the probable by merely applying *common sense* to the evidence. I doubt it. By definition, common sense is "the application of sound practical judgement concerning everyday matters that is shared by nearly all people." It may seem that some inherent insight about the truth of a given conclusion does "makes sense." But actually common sense is not as rock-solid as we might think it is. Why? Because it is a way of thinking influenced by time. For example, in the late twentieth century, it was a "commonsense" technological decision by an engineer to use diesel-powered cranes to raise the superstructure of

San Francisco's Transamerica Pyramid building. It made no "common sense" for the twentieth-century contractors to use thousands of manual laborers to construct earth ramps so that they could physically push the building materials up into place. This labor-intensive process may have been a commonsense decision in 2560 BC to build the Great Pyramids, but not the Transamerica building 4560 years later.

So just "common sense" applied to conclusions about the past cannot predominantly help us sort out the possible from the probable. That is not to confuse common sense with logic. Logic does not change with time. For example, regardless of time both the ancient Egyptian and modern architects did apply the same *logical* process to solve their construction challenges. In both cases, they had to find a source of energy to overcome gravity in order to move heavy objects to a certain elevated position. In this sense then, logic is really a timeless process, while common sense is a time-sensitive and actually a culturally determined opinion. Thus, it would seem that in historical archaeology, logic could indeed play a vital role in sorting the possible from the probable while common sense probably would not.

In fact, in the process of historical archaeology, logic can, in some cases, lead to knowledge of the past that is *almost certainly* true. For example, accounts written about the disastrous 1609–1610 winter where 80 percent of the Jamestown population starved to death emphatically reported instances of survival cannibalism. These references written by Jamestown officials and in one case, a Spanish ambassador, were quite graphic. But for years these stories seemed to me to be fabricated by people harboring a number of ulterior motives. One account written by the Governor, George Percy, I thought was made up in order to force the Virginia Company in London to quickly send more provisions to Virginia so that the colonists could spend less time searching for and growing food and more time prospecting for gold. The Spanish ambassador's account seemed to me to be written just to goad King James into dissolving the sponsoring Virginia Company and to recalling the colonists. This would end what the Spanish ambassador to England thought was the threat of English raids on Spanish gold fleets from a base at Jamestown. These explanations supported my underlying belief that the English would never resort to living off their own dead.

I was not the only one to discount these horrific stories. Dr. Rachel Herrman made a compelling documentary case that cannibalism during the starving time was very unlikely:

Historians need to reconsider cannibalism in Jamestown because the sources they draw on to describe the Starving Time are not transparent: 65 John Rolfe, 'A True Relation of the State of Virginia,' in Haile, Jamestown Narratives, 865–77 (quotation, 866). 66 Edward Williams, Virgo Triumphans, Or, Virginia In Generall, (London, 1650), 44. 67 Robert Beverley, The History and Present State of Virginia, ed. Louis B. Wright (Chapel Hill, N.C., 1947), 17 35 Of the five main authors [who mentioned cannibalism]—Gates, Percy, Smith, Strachey, and the Virginia Assembly—only one was present during the winter of 1609–10, and he did not claim to witness cannibalism. Furthermore the artfulness of Percy's account and what he had to lose in the way of honor and personal reputation if no one believed his story raise questions about its credibility as a reliable source. All the other writers had suspect motives for writing, which certainly may have affected the way they described events: Gates did not want to be implicated in the colony's near defeat and so denied starvation as well as man-eating, Smith was a self-promoting braggart, Strachey wanted to justify his involvement in propounding Lavves Diuine, Morall and Martiall, and the Virginia Assembly borrowed stories of the Starving Time to smear unrelated events. The numerous discrepancies among versions make it impossible to determine for certain what actually happened in Virginia.

(Rachel B. Herrman The William and
Mary Quarterly, Vol. 68, No. 1 (January 2011), pp. 47–74)

As it turned out, we were both *wrong*. Our excavations in the center of James Fort uncovered a cellar above a well next to a filled-in bakery cellar. Records suggested these cellars were in use from 1608 until they we abandoned just after the 1609–1610 starving time. Artifacts dating to that period were found "sealed" in the bakery cellar and the adjacent cellar/well. They included the butchered bones of horses, dogs, rats, and snakes, all indicating the remains of food eaten during a famine. Much to our surprise, in with these signs of stress, was a mutilated human skull and severed human leg bone. This combination of the archaeological context and the documentary evidence began to strongly suggest violence and even cannibalism. Then forensic analysis of the remains determined that the bones of this dead person were "processed" by chopping and fileting flesh off the bone and cracking and prying open the skull to remove the brain. There could be no other reasonable (logical) explanation for removing all this soft tissue except that these remains were butchered in a desperate attempt to stay alive. So in this case the convergence of field archaeology, history, and scientific evidence led to an "almost certain" conclusion that the historical accounts of survival cannibalism were not exaggerated.

But even with time-tested logic, let us consider a hypothetical example of how complicated it is to even almost certainly come close to gaining true knowledge through applied historical archaeology. Let's say in 1607, soldiers at Jamestown dug a narrow trench deep into virgin clay subsoil to plant a solid side-by-side log fort wall. The next year a fire that destroyed the wall left a layer of charcoal over the wall trenches. Then the fort was rebuilt. The site was then abandoned and became a farm which resulted in years of soil disturbance from plowing. Finally, the fort location became a museum and a public park during which plans were made to archaeologically investigate it to see if anything remained of the fort below ground.

To do that, archaeologists would have to peel back the layers of soil that had accumulated over 400 years. First, they would find the most recent deposit, the

blanket of soil blended together by park visitor traffic over the years (level A). Below that plowed soil was a deposit created by the years when the site was farmed
(level B). This plowed soil covered layers of "fallout" from people living in, drop-
ping things, and dying in the fort during the early seventeenth century (level C).
Under that lay burned wood (C) above streaks of mixed soil in a trench with signs
of decayed wooden posts (lay D). Nearby a cluster of graves was found some in
line with the wall trench (layer(s) E). If one then considers *logically*, how A relates
to B and B to C, C to D, and D to E, then it follows inevitability that D/E is the
oldest level. Consequently, with the 1607 "scene" so exposed (D/E), we can have
an almost eye-witness view of the scene that in 1607 documents tell us, the fort
was built with palisaded walls in just 19 days. The records also say this construction which took place often amid incoming Virginia Indian arrows caused a rash
of deaths among the first colonists. We can *imagine* the scene. By this process, we
have reached back in time and arrived at the *probability* of *true* knowledge. We
crossed the red line.

Put another way, the historical archaeology excavation process is not unlike
trying to discover how a traditional watch works by taking it apart and reassembling it. Obviously, first we would have to open the watch case and then part
by part repeat the watchmaker's meticulous assembly procedure in reverse. To
make this analogous to the A B C D E archaeological process outlined above,
we would consider that the watch is not unlike the site and the parts not unlike
artifacts imbedded in it. The first step of course would be to delicately open the
case. It should go without saying we would hardly open it with a hammer. And
similarly, an archaeologist would not haphazardly chew into a site with heavy
excavation machinery destroying the time-generated layers of soil it holds. The
watch would have to be dismantled by determining whatever parts are logically
fastened OVER or CONNECTED to other parts then removing them sequentially. So too the archaeological process first requires careful removal of its parts.
Again, they are topsoil, layer A, with whatever method would reveal the intact
and sealed layers below. Then archaeological layers B, C, D, E, etc. would be
removed from top to bottom.

Back to the watch analogy. If reassembling the watch was our goal in the end,
all the removed parts would have to be labeled sequentially, A, B, C, D, E, etc.
so they could go together again. Hopefully, if we were careful enough, we would
finally be able to put our labeled parts back together and have a functional watch
once again. In the process, we would have learned how and why the watch works.
By the same token, by systematically dismantling the archaeological site and hy-
pothetically reassembling it, we would be able to learn how the site was formed
over time. So the big payoff in both procedures is recapturing what happened in the
PAST, step by step, backward but then forward in time and space. At that point, we
could ask broader questions. For the watch, we could ask why people in the near
past needed to tell time at all and in the case of the analogous archaeological site
why our site "happened." But to understand our two collections of artifacts, we

must call into play wherever historical and scientific evidence is relevant. Then, it seems to me, we "likely" gain meaning and true knowledge. However, the watch analogy story can only go so far to explain the archaeology process unless it was clogged with A–E layers of "dirt" for a long time. In that case, some parts would be shuffled around and corroded away, ruling out a perfect reconstruction. So it is in Historical Archaeology.

In any event, on our hypothetical archaeological site these layers, A–E, were visible only to the trained eye. So what is a trained eye? That is simply one that can "read" the soil, learning by experience to perceive differing patterns of soil color, texture, and/or inclusions of cultural and natural material. This is actually both a logical and an aesthetic exercise. The aesthetic part is not unlike sorting through and comparing works of art. There seems to be no other way to read the differences between these unintentional dirt "canvases" (stratigraphy) created by human activity or occasionally human activity effected by natural events. Put another way, this requires the artistic ability of archaeologists to "see" certain logical design in stratigraphic layers in order to get some sense of how and why they were created. So the historical archaeologist must recognize patterns of soil tone, tactility, and/or composition of materials.

At Jamestown, there is no better example of this than the study of the many periods of burials on the site interred over time in the 1617 timber church and in its replacement church on the same site in 1639–1647 with a brick structure. By "seeing" the like and unlike visual patterns left in the soil that filled burial shafts, time passing can be sorted out. For example, the timber church burials would contain very little or no architectural material, while the burials dating after 1639–1647 would be littered with timber church destruction debris mixed with brick. In other words, this means to me that much of layered true knowledge in historical archaeology requires a certain talent for recognizing patterns that can be perceived at first as only subtle images. Scientific materials analysis may follow (see below).

But what about the historical part of historical archaeology: the role and use of historical records. Actually, it may seem, as most historians adamantly claim, that documentary history alone gets us to true knowledge of the past. That is not necessarily so according to this definition:

> I: History is the study of the human past as it is described in the written documents … but The past, with all its decisions completed, its participants dead and its history told, [is] what the general public perceives is ['an] the immutable bedrock on which we historians and archaeologists stand. But as purveyors of the past, we recognize that the bedrock is really quicksand … and …, bits of the story are yet untold …
>
> (K. Kris Hirst, archaeologist/journalist, February 28, 2017)

To me, the documentary past does not exactly stand on quicksand if one is aware of certain limitations. Written records are inherently illusive and fragmentary.

What to read, where to find it, how to read it, when to believe it and a whole host of other tests must be considered before accepting any account as truth. And beyond those caveats, a consideration must be made to determine how much was recorded incorrectly and/or incoherently and be cognizant of the possibility that little of the actual record survived; and of that, how much of the record cannot be found. Even if it could be found, there remains the imprecision of language. Word meaning often changes drastically through time. Remember "Discovery"? So given all those problems with documents then, do historical archaeologists throw them out? Quite the contrary. They are what they are and therefore should be critically included in the chain of evidence to play an *equal* role with our logic, art, and imagination. We just must admit that the written word is suspicious and needs to be rigorously analyzed as much as a layer of dirt.

But isn't historical archaeology a science? It is—sort of. But I think at best it is scientific. Why qualify this? Simply this, if one accepts the standard definition of science: "the intellectual and practical activity encompassing the systematic study of the structure and behavior of the physical and natural world through observation and 'experiment'," then there is a problem. While the historical archaeologist in practice does consider the "structure and behavior of the physical and natural world," he cannot exactly "experiment" with the world of the past. We cannot form a hypothesis and then test it by considering *all* the various combinations of variables from the past, to see if the hypothesis is valid. Why not? Because remember the variables are invisibly lurking behind the veil of the past. So we cannot know how to strictly include them in our quest for true knowledge. Again, the past has pasted. Nevertheless, the application of scientific analysis can be one more bullet in our archaeological arsenal to "approximate" true knowledge of the past.

In sum then, I believe historical archaeology necessarily requires a basic understanding of the theory and method of history, science, and art with a degree of educated imagination.

Having defined historical archaeology as the process of recovering and interpreting the remains of past human behavior through the discipline of history, science, art, and educated imagination, there remains to consider another vital step in the process, determining the reason(s) for doing it in the first place (the research design).

Doing historical archaeology can never be an end in itself. Randomly marching out on any ground anywhere to start digging would be a ridiculous exercise. As a means to an end, therefore, it is crucial that clear goals for the research are established before the shovel goes into the ground. In the scientific sense, a hypothesis must be adopted which answers the what, where, how, when, and why questions about whatever the effort hopes to learn about the past. Then an action is devised to test these questions. For example, long before our excavations began at Jamestown in 1994, I wrote a research design that was quite simple: to find the remains of the supposed lost three-sided 1607 Jamestown Fort in order to create a context for the documentary story of the founding of the Virginia Colony. I felt that would answer the "what" requirement. The "where" was defined by documentary research to an area "around" the only above-ground remnant of seventeenth-century Jamestown, a brick church tower. The "how" was to find the signs in the soil of three lines of trenches that formed a triangle. In the process, the "when" would be determined by early seventeenth-century dates of artifacts found sealed in these and other stratigraphically related 'Fort' deposits. Then my broad answer to "why" would be clear, simply to attempt to recapture the early seventeenth-century Jamestown natural and built landscape, that is, the backdrop where documentary history recorded the events in the lives of Englishmen, Powhatan native Americans, and enslaved Africans four centuries ago.

As it turned out, a research design this broad guided the Jamestown Rediscovery Archaeological Project research for 25 years, 1994–2020.

BIBLIOGRAPHY

Barber P., *The Complete Works of Captain John Smith* (University of North Carolina Press, London, 1986).

Berkeley W., *A Discourse and View of Virginia* (1663).

Billings W., *Sir William Berkeley, Dictionary of Virginia Biography* II, Library of Virginia, Richmond, 2001).

Billings W., *Sir William Berkeley* (Louisianna State Universite, Baton Rouge, 2004).

Carlson J., *Preliminary Report: Analysis of the Horse Skeleton Recovered from Jamestown Island* (Virginia College of William and Mary, MSS Jamestown Rediscovery, 2017).

Carson C., *Structure 144, MSS Report* (Association for the Preservation of Virginia Antiquities, n.d.).

Chamberlain J., "Pocahontas in London" The National Archives, catalogue reference, (Sp14/90 f.56).

Coombes J., *Feeding the "Machine" The Development of Slavery and Slave Society in Colonial Virginia* (Dissertation College of William and Mary).

Cotter J., *Archeological Excavations at Jamestown Virginia* (Washington, DC: National Park Service, 1958).

Deetz E., *Interim Report, Jamestown Rediscovery Archaeological Project mss.* Jamestown Rediscovery Foundation, 2002–2002).

Desandrouin N., Rochambeau Collection #57, Library of Congress.

Dorman J., *Adventurers of Purse and Person* (Geneological Pulishing Co., Baltimore, 2004.

Givens D., *Church and State: The Archaeology of the Foundations of Democracy, 1619–2019* (Carter Printing C., Richmond, VA, 2020).

Goodall J., *Virginia Academy of Science, "The Impact of Climate Change on Virginia"* (Washington, DC, 2005).

Gookin W., *Bartholomew Gosnold* (Achton Books, London, 1963).

Gravenhage Colectie Leupe, *Algemeenrijkarchief* (The Hague, n.d.).

Grizzard F., and Smith, D., *Jamestown Colony, a Political, Social, and Cultural History* (Greenwood Publishing Co., Westport, CT, 2007).

Haile E., *Jamestown Narratives* (RoundhouseChamplain, VA, 1998).

Henning W., *Statutes at Large* (1823).

Home County Magazine (London, 1889).

Hume I., *Martin's Hundred* (Knoph, New York, 1991).

Hume I., *A Guide to the Artifacts of Colonial America* (1970).

Ives P., *The Practice of Fortification* (London, 1589).

Journals of the House of Burgess (1619–1659).

Kaywood L., *Report on the Excavations at the Site of the Third Ridge* ... (MSS Colonial National Historic Park, 1954).

Kelso W., and Straube B., *Jamestown Rediscovery VIII* (Carter Printing, Richmond, VA, 2004).

Kelso W., *Jamestown, the Truth Revealed* (University of Virginia Press, Charlottesville, VA, 2017).

Kelso W., *Kingsmill Plantations, 1619–1800*, (Academic Press Inc., San Diego, 1984).

Kelso W., *The Buried Truth* (University of Virginia Press, Charlottesville, VA, 2006).

Kingsbury S., *The Records of the Virginia Company* (Government Printing Company, Washington, DC, 1933).

Lossing B., *The Pictorial Field-Book of the Revolution* (Harper and Brothers, New York, 1859).

Luccketti N., *Jamestown Rediscovery IV* (Carter Printing, Richmond, 1998).

May J., *Report on the Statehouse Excavations, MSS* (Jamestown Rediscovery, 2005).

McCartney M., *Jamestown Archaeological Assessment* (Colonial Nations Historical Park, Williamsburg, VA, 1998).

Morgan E., *American Slavery, American Freedom* (W.W. Norton Books, New York, 1975).

Mossiker F., *Pocahontas: Her Life and Legend* (Random House, New York, 1976).

Neville J., *Bacon's Rebellion, Abstracts of Materials in the Public Records Project* (The Jamestown Foundation, Richmond, n.d).

Notes on Ceremonial from the Ancient English Office Books, Directions for...Funerals, (London, 1888).

Percy G., *Observations Gathered Out of "Discourse of the Plantation of the Southern Colony by the English, 1606 written by the Honarble George Percy"*, ed. David B. Quinn (Association for The Preservation of Virginia Antiquities, Charlottesville, VA, 1967).

Pocock R., *The History of Gravesend and Milford* (Gale Publishers, Farmington, Michigan, n.d.).

Reps J., *Tidewater Towns* (Colonial Williamsburg Foundation, Williamsburg, VA, 1972).

Riley W., *New Town Property Report. MSS* (Jamestown Rediscovery Foundation, n.d.).

Robert P., *Richmond Dispatch* (Richmond, 1881).

Sainsbury W., *Calendar of State Papers, Colonial Series* (London, 1880).

Sanford P., *Subfloor Pits and the Archaeology of Slavery in Colonial Virginia* (Alabama Press, Tuscaloosa, 2007).

Shiner J., *Report on the Excavation in the Area of the Statehouse...*, MSS (Colonial National Historic Park, 1955).

Shutty M., *Bent, Holed and Folded* (Wasteland Press, Shelbyville, KY, 2019).

Tension E., *Elizabethan England: Being the History of this Country in Relation to all Foreign Princes* (Dove with Griffin, Warwick, Great Britain, 1936).

Thomas C., *Ye True Narrative of ye Princess Pocahontas* (Matoaka) (Press of Smither Brothers, 1897).

Thorpe, J., *Registrum Roffense, or, "A Collection of Antient Records, Charters, and Instruments of Divers Kinds: Necessary for Illustrating the Ecclesiastical History and Antiquities of the Diocese and Cathedral Church of Rochester"* 1682–1750., (Cambridge University Press, n.d.).

"Virginia under John Harvey," *Virginia Magazine of History and Biography*, Vol III (Virginia Historical Societh, Richmond, VA,1895).

Webb S., *1676 The End of American Independence* (Syracuse University Press, Syracuse New York 1996).

Whiffen M., *The Eighteenth Century Houses of Williamsburg* (Colonial Williamsburg Foundation, Williamsburg, VA, 1960).

Worthington M. *The Tree-Ring Dating of Timbers from St. Luke's Church, Smithfield, Isle of Wight County, Virginia* (unpublished report, 2008).

Wright L., *William Strachey. A True Reportory, Two Narratives* (Hakluyt Society Society, London, 1953).

Yonge, S. *The Site of Old "James Towne, 1607–1698"* (L.H. Jenkins, Richmond, VA, 1904).

INDEX

Note: Page references in *italics* denote figures and with "n" endnotes.

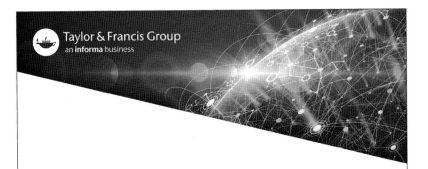